career pathways series

Avon's Career Pathways Series is for students, their parents, teachers and counselors, and is designed to enhance students' educational experience, focus career development, and inform educators and parents about ways to assist young people in making important decisions about educational and career choices now—and for the future.

ENDORSEMENTS FOR THE
CLASSROOM TEACHER'S WORKBOOK
FOR CAREER EDUCATION

"A complete and essential guide for all educators—resources, activities and ideas galore. A must for teachers who want to help their students make intelligent career choices . . . comprehensive and stimulating."

> William Jacob Bechem
> Teacher of Mathematics
> Greenwich, Connecticut

"*The Classroom Teacher's Workbook for Career Education* will serve as a real boost in enhancing the *practical* uses of foreign language study."

> Beverly A. Thomas
> Teacher of French
> Norwalk, Connecticut

ABOUT THE AUTHOR

JOYCE SLAYTON MITCHELL is an educational consultant, former school counselor, and writer in the field of career development and decision-making. She received an A.B. degree from Denison University and an M.S. degree from the University of Bridgeport. She is the author of *Free To Choose: Decision Making For Young Men*, *Other Choices For Becoming A Woman*, *The Work Book: A Guide To Skilled Jobs*, and *I Can Be Anything: Careers and Colleges for Young Women*.

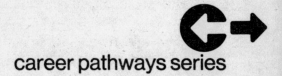

career pathways series

THE CLASSROOM TEACHER'S WORKBOOK FOR CAREER EDUCATION

by Joyce Slayton Mitchell

AVON
PUBLISHERS OF BARD, CAMELOT AND DISCUS BOOKS

THE CLASSROOM TEACHER'S WORKBOOK FOR CAREER EDUCATION is an original publication of Avon Books. This work has never before appeared in book form.

AVON BOOKS
A division of
The Hearst Corporation
959 Eighth Avenue
New York, New York 10019
Copyright © 1979 by Joyce Slayton Mitchell
Published by arrangement with the author.
Library of Congress Catalog Card Number: 79-65533
ISBN: 0-380-45179-4

First Avon Printing, August, 1979

SOURCES AND ACKNOWLEDGMENTS

The primary source of information for *The Classroom Teacher's Workbook for Career Education* is the resource library of the Office of Career Education in the United States Department of Education. These library materials included a government grant project which resulted in the publication which was central to this book, *Career Guidance in the Arts and Humanities, A Career Exploration Series*, GPO, 1976.

In addition, the many position papers of Dr. Kenneth B. Hoyt, Director of the Office of Career Education, provided the guidelines and principles from which the career education activities in this book were developed. Other materials from the resource library which were of particular value were the career education programs developed by state departments of education in California, North Carolina, North Dakota and Oklahoma.

The major source of information for the special groups materials is the Council on Interracial Books for Children, and materials developed from a 1977 government grant project which resulted in the publication, *Guidance, Counseling, and Support Services for High School Students with Physical Disabilities*.

The curriculum charts with related careers are from the United States Department of Education.

I want to thank the Director of Career Education, Ken Hoyt, for his concern for career education in the classroom and his special interest in this project. Thanks also to Sid High in the Office of Career Education for time spent helping me in the resource library in Washington.

I am grateful to Linda Magoon for developing her typing skills to include typing in columns, drawings, and charts which were required for this manuscript.

Thanks to Lyla Hoffma, CIBC, for permission to use the materials from the Resource Center of Racism and Sexism.

To Sue Coil at Avon, I am indebted for her enthusiasm for a classroom teacher's guide before this project even began.

I want to express my appreciation to my editor, Jean Feiwel, for her good content suggestions and her sharp sense of design.

Joyce Slayton Mitchell   Wolcott Vermont
                                           February 14, 1979

CONTENTS

TO THE CLASSROOM TEACHER

Career education is sweeping the country. Many of you will be asked by your principal, or department head, or maybe some parents what you are doing about career education.

Most of you aren't looking for something new to add to your curriculum. Most of you know the benefits of your own subject matter and you can use all the time you can get to teach that subject. Most of you have students leaving your classroom for sports, the school band, college recruiters, field trips, and testing and it seems as though your students are never there to learn what you have to teach.

Career education may be the last thing you want to take on. If this is the case, *The Classroom Teacher's Workbook for Career Education* is designed for you. It's written for the teacher who feels that there just isn't time in a busy schedule for career exploration (or any other latest fad on the educational bandwagon). The book is purposely *not* loaded down with concepts of career education (you will probably get those in in-service training in your own school), with essays (you have enough to read with your own class preparation), nor does it contain more than you want to know about career education.

The purpose of the book is to give you, the classroom teacher, *activities* that will enable you to integrate the notion of making money (which all students will eventually have to do) with your subject matter. In addition there are general activities for those of you who do want to do more with career education, and for some of you who may want to do more for a general career education program in the school. But primarily, all you have to do to fulfill your career education responsibilities to your students and your supervisors is to skim over the introduction to find out what career education is and what you can do about it, and then turn to the section on your own subject matter and there follow the activities and exercises that seem best to work for you.

9

To supplement your basic classroom activities you may want to send for, or get from your school library, the suggested resources for your classroom. You can also expand your program by assigning a "career plan workbook" for each of your students. This workbook can be a manila folder or a loose-leaf notebook containing the exercises you do in class and the outside assignments you give. You can reproduce the exercises in Phase I—"About the Student"—and use them as the basic starting point of the student's workbook. Material drawn from interviews with working people, reading reports, and the exploration of careers within your subject matter can also be included in these workbooks.

Another resource to supplement your program that you may want to consider is the contribution that parents can make. As prime influencers of their children's values and decisions, parents can be tremendously helpful to your career education efforts. You can ask them to give a clear account of their work to their children. This will help the children understand both the nature and the social significance of their parents' work (both paid and unpaid).

Parents can provide opportunities within their home and family structure for their children to experience work—as a family member—in ways that both help the family and enable the student to understand his own contribution to the well-being of the family as a social unit. Students can learn skills working at all of the necessary jobs within the home. Often in families where both parents have a career the children learn about work as a family member, but when one of the parents is usually at home, children often lose out on this accessible work environment. When everyone contributes to the family work—especially the menial tasks of cleaning up, picking up, garbage, and vacuuming, the children learn that all jobs have their dull routine sides. This necessary routine work becomes bearable, however, as each family member contributes.

Parents can also help their children understand and appreciate the career implications that your subject matter represents by the homework you have assigned. Your communication to parents about these issues at a parents' school event or a written memo sent home can lead to the necessary connections for students and their parents.

Career Education, What Is It?

Career education, for the classroom teacher, is a plan to tie in curriculum with the student's career development. Career means both paid and unpaid work. A career, as it is understood and used in career education, is every job—or all the work—that a person does in a lifetime. Therefore, your students' work right now in school is their career. A summer job, or an after-school voluntary job at the scouts, or a regular job at home is also a part of a student's present career. It is important for students to understand that all the work they do counts as part of their career development. In that way, work in education, military service, child-rearing, home management, community service as well as paid work on a regular job are all part of a person's career. These work situations are valuable because in all of them people learn skills that empower them to widen their career options.

Basic Assumptions of Career Education

Since everything counts in one's career development and since a person's education extends from preschool through the retirement years, career education is a lifelong process. Career education is for everyone—including all ages, the mentally disabled, the intellectually gifted, the poor, the rich, the physically disabled, the nondisabled, female, male, students in elementary school and in graduate school. The sooner students see themselves in a career developmental process, the sooner their present education will become more meaningful to them— as will their summer work experiences, family work, and after-school work experiences.

It's especially important that young women see the value in career education because so many cultural influences have given them the false impression that they won't need to make money. Young women get the message that if all goes well, they will be financially taken care of by someone else. They are led to believe that they probably will not be financially supporting others. The facts are that only 7 percent of all American families have a Dick and Jane version of the father as breadwinner, the mother at home with the two kids, while almost as many (6.2 percent or over 8 million families!) are headed solely by women. It's about time that we as educators act on the assumption that it's crucial for young women to prepare in school, like their brothers do, to make money.

The basic assumptions, then, are that career education is for everyone, and that it's a lifelong learning process.

Components of Career Education

An orientation to occupations and careers in your subject matter is a main component of career education in your classroom. Besides that, students need to have a general understanding of our economic system, an awareness of themselves and the world of work. Some students will want the chance for in-depth exploration of selected careers within your field of study. The research and exploration activities cited later in the book can be used for the in-depth component. Another possible component is for the students to learn about the educational preparation necessary for the careers they explore. The basic resources to help you with this component are cited under "Educational Pathways" on page 67.

Goals for Students in Career Education

Goals you can expect within your classroom include competency in the basic content skills of your subject matter. Students also can learn transferable skills in your classroom such as good study habits and decision-making skills and the ability to acquire a degree of self-understanding through your classroom work. They can expect to become aware of ways to find meaningful occupation through work in your field. They can also learn something of the means available for continuing their education, for changing career directions, and about careers related to those in your subject matter.

Career Education, Do We Need It?

Now that we know what career education is, do we need it? It is a rare school that equips all its students to make the choice upon graduation of entering the job market with a salable skill or of continuing their education. Too often the graduate has neither possibility, let alone the opportunity to select one or the other.

Nearly 2.5 million students leave the formal education system of the United States each year without adequate preparation for a job. In a modern society, formal education stands directly between students and their ability to support themselves and their families. If the quality or the appropriateness of any student's formal education is poor, what might have been a pathway to opportunity will remain a barrier. To fail to fulfill a responsibility in this respect means that many of the future citizens of this country will end up economically obsolete.

If we are to prepare students for responsible adulthood we must initiate career education as a developmental process toward the awareness of meaningful work in their life. Every student needs the skills for meaningful work. Do we need career education? We need it!

What Can You, the Classroom Teacher, Do About Career Education?

Start with your own subject matter, your own students. *The Classroom Teacher's Workbook* is designed to help you integrate your program with career education. The basic assumption of the book is that students will learn more about work by activities and exercises in their classrooms than·in a special unit on career education. They learn as they ask you, "What am I studying this for?" Or as they say, "I love or hate this subject!"

No special number of units is planned because you can integrate the three parts of career education—1) about the student, 2) about work, 3) educational pathways to connect student and work—in many different directions. You can focus on the student or on work or on educational pathways depending on your subject and grade level and interests. Often the guidance department focuses on the student while the classroom teachers concentrate on work as it relates to the subject they are teaching. Or you can focus on the student in a special unit or a unit on educational pathways as it relates to your subject matter.

Using the Workbook

If you decide to do some career development work with your students, start with the activities on pages 16–42, "About the Student–Phase I." You can duplicate the activities, assign them, have the students take the assignments home, or do the work in your classroom, or assign the activities to be completed and put in their career planning notebooks. You can use the results of their activities for class discussion, small group discussions, with parents, in student–parent conferences, or ask the student to discuss the results at home with their parents or at school with their counselor for career planning.

Start with Activity 1, for example, "Here I Am, World!" for the first assignment toward the goal of student awareness to be completed, discussed at home, and kept in their career notebooks. In addition, you may assign Activity 3 ("Self-rating"), Activity 6 ("Values Voting"), or all or one or none of the activities in this section. How you use and integrate the activities with your classwork depends on your own goals and time.

For many of you, a few activities concerning the student and some concerning work as it relates to your discipline, with follow-up work in educational pathways for the student to figure out where she can get the necessary preparation, will be an appropriate use of these materials. The general work you do with your students in the three phases of career development can then be made more specific by turning to classroom strategies, pages 78–166, which are activities designed especially for your subject matter. Use these activities for in-depth career exploration.

Special materials for special groups of students are on pages 167–187. There are special students in all schools. Five percent of all school-aged children are gifted and talented, one in eleven (9 percent) of the population has a physical disability, and the majority of the population (over 50 percent) are female and nonwhite. Assuming that career education is for everyone in the school, students will get more out of the career ed curriculum if teachers are aware of the latest resources for special groups.

The Classroom Teacher's Workbook for Career Education is designed for you to pick and choose and build in whatever ways fit your teaching needs. One more thing that may help before you begin—every subject has its own talk—here is a little

Career Education Talk

Many terms will be used in this workbook in discussing career education. When you think of a "career" you may think of a one-job, full-time profession: a career in law, a career in education, and so on. Would you include a person's part-time hospital volunteer job as part of his or her career? Would you consider a student's night-time waitressing or waiter's job as part of a career? Well, career educators would.

Here are definitions of some terms used throughout the workbook.

Career All the work, paid or unpaid, full-time or part-time, that a person does in a lifetime. A career is made up of paid work, volunteer work, student work, military service, education, apprenticeship training, or any experience defined as work in any place where a person learns and manages skills. Career starts in early childhood education and extends through retirement.

Occupation A group of related activities or tasks that are a person's "title." (What do you do, or what is your occupation? I am a teacher. I am an economist.)

Job Usually a more specific term than occupation. (What is your job? I am a math teacher. As an economist, I am a financial analyst for Allied Chemicals.)

Task A specific activity performed on the job. (I write letters. I punch computer cards. I talk on the phone to clients.)

Setting Place of work. (School, factory, museum, government agency.)

Field A group of jobs with similar focus that sometimes require similar skills—the humanities field, the social science field, the field of history, or sports, or mathematics.

Skill A developed aptitude or ability.

Transferable skills Skills people use over and over in a great variety of activities. Speaking, writing, decision making, time-management, persistence, and persuasion skills, for example. Skills that are learned in any college major, at home, in a paying or volunteer job.

Content skills Skills relating to technical knowledge in one particular field, such as the mechanics of a car, the anatomy of the body, a foreign language, typing, or baseball skills. They are needed for a particular career or specific job and are often learned in a formal program.

CAREER DEVELOPMENT

There are three basic phases in students' career development. The first is to learn about themselves—to assess their skills, values, and interests. The second is to learn about work, or their career possibilities, and the third phase is to find the educational pathways that will lead them to where they want to go.

About the Student—Phase I

Phase I—about the student—includes activities, reading references, and films that will help students assess their interests, abilities, values, and goals. Although students change with learning and experience, carrying out the activities and reading assignments should help them decide what is important to them, what questions to ask, what information to consider in making decisions—now and later. The results of the activities can be used in future decision making, particularly if each student maintains a personal career plan workbook, containing forms, test scores, notes on occupational research, and so on.

Each of the activities and readings can be conducted independently or as part of a sequence in your classroom. Sessions with small groups of students offer the double benefit of using the leader's time efficiently and allowing students to interact. If used independently, an activity could serve as an introduction to other career education activities in your classroom or as a special project for an interested individual. Parents, other teachers, community volunteers, or students can assist with the research necessary for adapting the activities.

Exploring Oneself

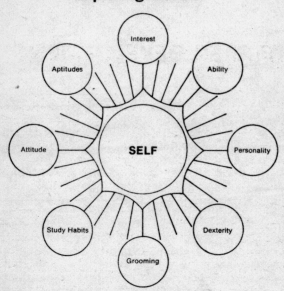

Activity 1: Here I Am, World!

Purpose: With this questionnaire, students can describe for themselves their general self-knowledge, achievements, limitations, interests, family, work values, physical characteristics, personality traits, risk-taking dimensions, and future plans.

Procedures: Reproduce from this workbook a questionnaire for each student, and include the questions at the end according to whether students are on the junior high level or senior high level. If the questionnaires are taken home to be filled out, students should answer the questions without assistance from family or friends.

Follow-up: The "Here I Am, World!" activity provides a useful base for career discussions. At your discretion, students can share some or all responses in a group setting. By keeping the questionnaire in a "career plan workbook," a student can note changes and new experiences upon progressing in school.

Here I Am, World!

NAME: _____ DATE: _____
AGE: _____ GRADE: _____

School-related Questions

1. What subjects do I like most? 1)_____ 2)_____ 3)_____
2. What subjects do I like least? 1)_____ 2)_____ 3)_____
3. In what subjects do I do my best work? 1)_____ 2)_____
   3)_____
4. In what subjects do I do my worst work? 1)_____ 2)_____
   3)_____
5. My study habits are ____excellent ____good ____fair
   ____poor.
6. My grades tell the story of how well I can do in school.
   ____Yes ____No If no, please explain: _____
   _____
7. I have participated in or am planning to participate in the
   following extracurricular activities: _____
   _____

Work-related Questions

8. When I was a child, I wanted to be a _____
9. **Now** I think I want to be a _____ (Check one of the
   following.) I am ____very sure, ____somewhat sure,
   ____unsure that this is a good choice for me.
10. Do I have to go to college to do this kind of work?____Yes
    ____No
11. I have had the following jobs (either for pay or without pay):
    a.   d.
    b.   e.
    c.   f.
    Underline the ones you enjoyed.
    Circle the ones you disliked.
12. An ideal job for me would have the following characteris-
    tics:
    a.
    b.
    c.
13. I will be unhappy if I find myself working in a job where I
    have to:
    a.
    b.
    c.

14. I hope I never have to work with people who are:
    a.
    b.
    c.
15. I think three reasons why people work are:
    a.
    b.
    c.

Leisure-related Questions

16. I like to do these activities in my free time:
    a.   d.
    b.   e.
    c.   f.
    Underline those you do alone.
    Circle your favorites.
17. I like to read the following kinds of books and magazines:
_____
18. I have taken or plan to take the following lessons outside of school: _____
19. If I had one full day to do anything I want, I would: ____
_____

Family-related Questions

20. My family wants me to be a ____ to make a living. I think this is ____ a good idea ____ a bad idea ____ I am not sure. Please explain _____
_____
21. My family feel that I ____should ____should not go to college.
22. Which of my qualities or habits does my family want me to change?
_____
_____

General Questions

23. My health is ____excellent ____good ____fair ____poor.
24. My energy level is ____high ____medium ____low.
25. Do I have any physical disabilities that might limit my career or educational plans? For example, am I hard of hearing? _____
_____
26. Do I have any personality traits which might affect my choice of jobs? For example, am I shy, sociable, impatient, independent?_____
_____
27. What do I think is my best quality? _____

28. What personal quality would I most like to change? ____
_____

29. What am I most proud of having done or being able to do?
    a.
    b.
    c.

30. What are three of my weaknesses?
    a.
    b.
    c.

31. Am I willing to get involved with new ideas, friends, or situations, even if I don't know whether they will work out? ____ Yes ____ Sometimes ____ No

32. Up until now, what is the most important thing I know about myself? _____
_____

33. If my friends were to use one word or phrase to describe me, what would it be? _____

34. When I am old, what do I want people to say about me?
_____

35. If I weren't me, what other person (real or fictitious) would I choose to be? _____
    Why? _____
_____

Additional Questions for Junior High School Students

36. During high school, I plan to be in
    ____ the vocational program
    ____ the general program
    ____ the college preparatory program
    ____ the business program
    ____ the distributive education program
    ____ other _____
    ____ don't know

37. I **want** to select courses in these areas in high school:
    a.   d.
    b.   e.
    c.   f.

38. I plan to finish high school. ____ Yes ____ No
    If not, please explain: _____
_____

39. I would like to talk with a counselor about my career and educational plans. ____ Yes ____ No

Additional Questions for Senior High School Students

40. I plan to finish high school. ____ Yes ____ No
    If no, please explain: _____
_____

41. When I leave high school, the first thing I plan to do is:
    ____get apprenticeship training
    ____get a job
    ____get married and work
    ____get married and not work
    ____go into military service
    ____attend a 2-year college
    ____attend a 4-year college
    ____attend a technical or career school
    ____take time off before doing any of the above
    ____other_____
42. If I plan to go to college, it is because (check all that apply):
    ____my family expects me to
    ____my family will pay the bills
    ____it would be fun
    ____I want to learn more through formal academic courses
    ____I need to for the kind of work I am planning to do
    ____I don't want to begin steady work yet
    ____it is not too different from what I have been doing in high school
    ____I would like to live away from home
    ____I don't know much about other possibilities
    ____my friends are going
    ____other_____
43. I would like to talk with a counselor about my career and educational plans. ____Yes ____No

Activity 2: Here Is My Family and Community

1. Family occupations: Can you list the jobs of each of these persons in your family? (List only those in your particular family. All of the following may not apply to you. Substitute guardian or foster parents, if appropriate.)
   Father: _____
   Mother: _____
   Brothers: _____
   Sisters: _____
   Grandfather: _____
   Grandmother: _____
   Grandfather: _____
   Grandmother: _____
   Is there a pattern of occupations within your family? ____
   Which jobs are most alike? Why? Which jobs seem most different?

Why? _____
_____
_____
_____
_____
_____
_____

2. How did your parents choose their jobs?
Father: _____
Mother: _____

3. What types of preparation were necessary in your parents' careers? How did your parents prepare for their jobs?

	Mother	Father
Education? (What grade or special schooling?)	_____	_____
On-the-job training?	_____	_____
Apprenticeship?	_____	_____
Other?	_____	_____

4. List six industries in your community that employ twenty or more people:

_____ _____
_____ _____
_____ _____

5. Have you visited one of the industries? _____ Yes _____ No
Which ones?_____

6. Listed below are the eleven career clusters in the world of work. List an example of a job within each category.
Art, Design, & Communications: _____
Construction: _____
Health Services: _____
Mechanics & Repair:_____
Office & Clerical: _____
Sales Careers: _____
Science & Technology: _____
Service Careers: _____
Social Services & Education: _____
Trade & Industry: _____
Transportation: _____

7. What part-time jobs did your family have while attending school?
Mother: _____
_____
Father: _____
_____
Brothers:_____
Sisters: _____

8. Where can career information be secured?
1) _____
2) _____

9. List three ways you could gather information about an interesting career:
   1) _____
   2) _____
   3) _____
10. Have you ever investigated a job? _____ Yes _____ No
    If yes, what method did you use to locate your information?
    _____
11. Have you ever used a library card catalog to locate information about a career? _____ Yes _____ No
12. Have you ever talked with a person about his or her job? _____ Yes _____ No
    If yes, what was the job? _____
13. Have you ever thought of yourself as a person doing a job? _____ Yes _____ No
    If yes, what jobs? _____
14. All jobs relate to working with data, people, or things. A teacher, for example, works mainly with students, not data or things. A statistician works primarily with data, and an auto mechanic deals chiefly with things. If you were to choose today, which of these three would be most important to you in selecting an occupation? Explain why.
    _____
    _____
15. What do these words mean?
    1) Job: _____
    2) Career: _____
    3) Aptitude: _____
    4) Interests: _____
    5) Apprentice: _____
    6) Task: _____
16. What are your special interests? _____
    _____
17. What are your hobbies? _____
    _____
18. What things do you do best? _____
    _____
19. What part-time jobs have you had? _____
    _____
    _____
20. If you were to choose a job now, would you prefer to:
    _____ stay in your home community
    _____ stay in this area
    _____ stay in the state
    _____ move to another part of the country
21. Have you ever thought of your school record in terms of

later careers? _____ Yes _____ No
If yes, how? _____

22. How can you review your past school record for possible clues to future educational and career choices? _____
_____

23. What part-time job did you like the most? _____
_____

24. What part-time job did you like the least? _____
_____

Activity 3: Self-rating

Purpose: The following self-rating check list has been included for one purpose only—to stimulate students' appraisal of their personal qualities. No attempt has been made to provide an all-inclusive list that would serve as a crystal ball to foretell their future or to give them a scientific test with proven validity and reliability. The sole purpose is to stimulate their thinking.

Procedure: Students should be honest in rating themselves. If they truly think they are "Right up there," they should give themselves four points for that quality; "Better than O.K." deserves three points; "Less than O.K." two points; and "Not so good on this one" rates one point. Most people will probably score between 200 and 150.

Regardless of their score, they must examine each trait on which they scored less than three points with the aim of noticing anything that surprises them concerning that particular characteristic.

Directions: Rate yourself as honestly as you can on the qualities or skills listed in the groups below. Use this rating scale:

4 = Right up there.   2 = Less than O.K.
3 = Better than O.K.   1 = Not so good on this one.

How Would You Rate Your Ability To:

	Score			Score
1. Persuade others	___	11.	Read quickly & comprehend	___
2. Handle money	___	12.	Judge accurately	___
3. Take responsibility	___	13.	Originate ideas	___
4. Understand others' problems	___	14.	Make new	

5. Balance class work & activities-employment ___
6. Plan ___
7. Analyze problems ___
8. Speak effectively ___
9. Write clearly ___
10. Handle emergencies ___

acquaintances ___
15. Converse intelligently on a variety of subjects ___
16. Listen ___
17. Grow intellectually ___
18. Concentrate ___
19. Take the initiative ___
20. Lead others ___
TOTAL ___

How Would You Rate Your Personal Qualifications:

21. Usual health ___
22. Vitality ___
23. Appearance ___

24. Grooming ___
25. Emotional reactions (anger, nervousness) ___
TOTAL ___

How Would You Rate Your Willingness To:

26. Take orders from others ___
27. Carry out assigned tasks ___
28. Learn ___
29. Work ___
30. Smile ___
31. Be friendly ___
32. Be cooperative ___
33. Travel (when job requires it) ___

34. Speak to large groups ___
35. Offer suggestions ___
36. Admit you are wrong ___
37. Accept minority groups ___
38. Party ___
38. Spend money ___
40. Loaf ___
TOTAL ___

How Would You Rate Your Courage To:

41. Speak out when you know you are right ___

45. Fight for the "underdog" ___
46. Make a decision ___

Response Form for What's So Special about Me?

Statement #	Yes, This Is True	Unimportant
1.	_____	_____
2.	_____	_____
3.	_____	_____
4.	_____	_____
5.	_____	_____
6.	_____	_____
7.	_____	_____
8.	_____	_____
9.	_____	_____
10.	_____	_____
11.	_____	_____
12.	_____	_____
13.	_____	_____
14.	_____	_____
15.	_____	_____
16.	_____	_____
17.	_____	_____
18.	_____	_____
19.	_____	_____
20.	_____	_____
21.	_____	_____
22.	_____	_____
23.	_____	_____
24.	_____	_____
25.	_____	_____
26.	_____	_____
27.	_____	_____
28.	_____	_____
29.	_____	_____
30.	_____	_____
31.	_____	_____
32.	_____	_____
33.	_____	_____
34.	_____	_____
35.	_____	_____

No, This Is Not True	Corresponding Work Values
_____	_____
_____	_____
_____	_____
_____	_____
_____	_____
_____	_____
_____	_____
_____	_____
_____	_____
_____	_____
_____	_____
_____	_____
_____	_____
_____	_____
_____	_____
_____	_____
_____	_____
_____	_____
_____	_____
_____	_____
_____	_____
_____	_____
_____	_____
_____	_____
_____	_____
_____	_____
_____	_____
_____	_____
_____	_____
_____	_____

42. Defend minority
    groups   ___
43. Say "No"   ___
44. Ask for assistance
    & direction   ___

47. Plan your future   ___

                        TOTAL   ___

How Would You Rate Your:

48. Scholastic grades   ___
49. Record in solving
    problems   ___
50. Patience with others
    who have lesser
    abilities   ___
51. Tolerance of
    religious creeds   ___
52. Congeniality   ___
53. Sense of humor   ___
54. Maturity   ___
55. Attitude toward
    fellow students   ___
56. Inquisitiveness   ___

57. Decisiveness   ___
58. Initiative   ___
59. Understanding of
    your deficiencies &
    assets   ___
60. Appreciation of
    an education   ___
61. Honesty   ___
62. Confidence &
    poise   ___
63. Activities in school   ___
64. Activities in the
    community   ___

                   TOTAL: ___
                   Total Score: ___

Areas in which you might improve: _____
_____
_____

Your plan of action for improvement: _____
_____
_____
_____
_____

Activity 4: What's So Special About Me?

Purpose: Before planning their educational and occupational
future, students must understand the personal work values that

may act as motivating forces; therefore, this activity encourages students to view their own pattern of work values as expressed through their interests and experiences. Students should realize that their work values may change over time, and integrating them into their career decisions is a continuing process.

Because the range of work values is varied, the following list of behavioral statements and corresponding values is not intended to be definitive. The list contains suggestions that the teacher may change or supplement according to desire or need.

Procedure: At least two methods for conducting this exercise are possible: spontaneous group participation or individually recorded activity. In either case, the teacher should print each behavioral statement with its number on a card or large sheet of paper.

Spontaneous Group Participation
   a. The leader reads and shows each behavioral statement to students.
   b. Students must raise their hands high if the statement pertains to them, raise them to chest level if it is unimportant, or not raise their hands if it is untrue for them.
   c. If the teacher wishes, each student could write down the statement numbers to which he or she responded positively. The teacher should emphasize the importance of independent choices, regardless of the actions of other students.

Individually Recorded Activity
   a. The teacher reads and shows each behavioral statement to students.
   b. Using the response form, students check the appropriate box (Yes, this is true for me; Unimportant; or No, this is *not* true for me).

Upon completion, the teacher and students extrapolate in discussion the work value which corresponds to each behavioral statement. Students note on the form only those work values matching the statements chosen for importance.

Follow-up: The information provided by this exercise, especially when students have the response forms for reference, could lead to further career exploration.

Discussion could focus on individual patterns of work values.

Brainstorming could result in students mentioning jobs

that satisfy particular work values and conversely those jobs which are unlikely choices.

Students could develop charts headed by either work values or specific occupations and fill in the missing information.

Behavioral Statements	Corresponding Work Values
1. I like to work with my hands	Creating, fixing things
2. I like to solve intellectual problems	Working with ideas
3. I like to motivate others	Leadership/persuasion
4. I like to work with others	Teamwork
5. I like to be my own boss	Independence/autonomy
6. I like to help other people	Social responsibility
7. I like competition	Competitiveness/self-confidence
8. I like the challenge of different tasks	Variety
9. I do my best work during the day	9 to 5 hours
10. I want to make a lot of money	Material possessions/ambition
11. I want to have an interesting job	Satisfying work
12. I want to be able to dress as I like	Casualness/nonconformity
13. I want a job without hassles	Harmony/relaxation
14. I want a lot of time for leisure and family	Free time
15. I like to develop original ideas	Creativity
16. I like to stand out as an individual	Self-expression/recognition
17. I like making important decisions	Responsibility/power
18. I want to study after high school	Willingness to study/ self-discipline
19. I like to have other people see my work	Approval/recognition
20. I want to do the absolute best I can	Perfectionism/determination/ ambition
21. I like to coordinate ideas, people, and plans	Organization
22. I want to do something to benefit society	Social conscience
23. I like working with details	Precision

24. I want to be assured of having a job — Economic security
25. I try to be sincere and truthful — Honesty/integrity
26. I like to be the chairperson of a committee — Leadership/organization
27. I like to work with others on a committee — Teamwork/interest in people
28. I like to write for the school newspaper or magazine — Self-expression through writing
29. I like to manage school teams, performance groups — Organization/leadership
30. I like to draw for the school newspaper or magazine — Self-expression through art
31. I would like to be a member of Future Teachers of America — Social responsibility through teaching
32. I like to make scenery for the school play — Manual enjoyment/dexterity
33. I like to be in the school orchestra — Self-expression through music
34. I am willing to try out for a role in the school play — Self-confidence/self-expression through acting
35. I like to be on the decorations committee for school parties — Self-expression through art

Activity 5: Discussion Topics and Provocative Questions for Career Exploration

A. Discussion Topics

Individuals perceive different advantages and disadvantages in jobs.

For example, the axiom that "one person's meat is another person's poison" is true in discussing job satisfaction. Two people having the same job might have very different feelings about it. At this time it might be appropriate to discuss individual views of "success." Does it mean recognition, money, helping others?

Extracurricular and community activities can provide experiences that lead to reality testing of potential occupations.

For example, being an editor on the school newspaper forces one to deal with evaluating the work of others, coordinating both the creating and production aspects of publishing, and meeting deadlines.

People continue to change and grow.

For example, the person who at twenty-five is satisfied with his or her job as a salesperson may find that at thirty-five another kind of work would better suit his or her needs and abilities.

The world changes, and with change comes the need for individuals to adapt to new conditions.

For example, those workers who use art skills in graphic arts (printing) must adjust to technological advances in materials and machinery. Another example concerns the contraction of whole job fields, such as teaching, when the economic forces of supply and demand are at work.

Stereotyping jobs according to sex is detrimental.

For example, a young man might have the necessary attributes and the desire to become a nurse, but negative comments from his parents and friends might deter him.

Work environment plays a role in job choice.

For example, a person who likes being associated with the theater might choose to apply her skills as a sound or light technician in that setting rather than at a television station.

There are different kinds of work within every career field.

For example, there are four divisions within each arts field. These include many kinds of workers related to the overall field. Representative occupations in music, for instance, include:
    Performance — musician
    Production — recording engineers
    Business and management — concert manager
    Education — music teacher

Individuals work to satisfy different needs.

> For example, one person may want to work as little as possible to survive. Some people work at distasteful chores to support a hobby, such as photography. Sometimes work fulfills so many needs that there is little time and desire for family life and leisure pursuits.

Learning does not end when work begins.

> For example, a lawyer must keep abreast of changes in laws that affect her practice.

Every occupation has disadvantages as well as advantages.

> For example, a television performer or backstage technician may have to rise very early or stay up late at night. Personnel in airlines and health jobs have to work on shifts because services are available seven days a week, twenty-four hours a day.

B. Provocative Questions

Does society, in general, reward people (with money or status) according to whether their work benefits other people?

> For example, why aren't teachers more highly paid and considered at the top of prestige scales?

Why are people who work with their hands usually paid less than those who work with ideas?

> For example, drafters are paid less than architects. Is this strictly a matter of education? How have unions been important in equalizing this kind of discrepancy in other areas, such as music?

What are some of the basic reasons why a person might want to devote his working life to the arts or humanities?

> For example, in the arts there is often opportunity for self-expression, creativity, and recognition. The humanities might satisfy individual needs to indulge intellectual curiosity, help others, or provide insight into our cultural past, present, and future.

What is the relationship between talent and success?

> For example, will an artist who produces superb work be recognized if he or she makes no effort to find an audience?

What is the relationship between performance occupations and business occupations? Do the latter exploit the performers or do they provide useful services?

> For example, a literary agent knows which publishers might accept a writer's work and helps arrange business affairs. The agent's work leaves time for the writer to concentrate on writing, but also costs the writer a fee.

Does making a lot of money necessarily mean a happier life?

> For example, does the successful copyright lawyer enjoy life more than the poet who clerks in a bookstore to support his poetry writing?

Could computers or robots do the jobs of most workers?

> For example, automation could take over the instructional duties of a teacher, but it could never replace the active thinking or personal relationships necessary in teaching. Also, cameras can take pictures, but only human filmmakers can develop a special theme or vision to make the movie significant.

Activity 6: Values Voting

Purpose: This exercise provides a quick method for introducing values issues into a classroom study unit or discussion and for eliciting individual and group responses. It also provides some indication of where everyone "stands," and it offers opportunities for the individual to practice making public declarations.

Procedure: The teacher or a class member announces the "issues" to be voted upon from a prepared list. As each item is announced, the class votes, nonverbally, by raising hands to indicate agreement and by pointing thumbs down to indicate disagreement. Uncertainty or neutrality may be shown by folded arms. The strength of opinion can be indicated by vigorous waving of hands or by the pumping up and down of the "thumbs down" sign. The exercise can be introduced periodically, using different lists. The lists should not always be prepared by the teacher; student input should be encouraged.

The following suggested list covers some work and career attitudes. It is by no means exhaustive.

1. Without a college degree you "just don't get no respect."
2. Anyone with enough brains to do it should figure out some way to make a living that doesn't involve punching a time clock.
3. Just about anyone can learn a craft or trade such as plumbing or carpet laying or cement finishing.
4. I would be embarrassed ten to fifteen years from now to have to tell those who are currently my best friends that I still make a living with my hands.
5. Workers and wage earners would be victimized by employers if it weren't for labor unions.
6. Labor unions just encourage laziness, waste, and the attitude that you ought to get away with anything you can on the job.
7. Life isn't worth living if the work you are doing is boring.
8. Someone must do the hard, dirty, or boring work in our society, but it sure isn't going to be me!
9. If a person thinks about it and really tries to do his or her best, that person can get satisfaction even from a job that nobody else wants.
10. It doesn't really matter how hard you try. If the boss doesn't take a liking to you, you'll get stuck with the dirty work forever.
11. Once you get in bad with someone on the job, there's nothing you can do to change that opinion of you, and you might as well leave.
12. The only way you can be happy in your job is if you find one that fits your individual interests and abilities.
13. If you try too hard to turn out good work rapidly, they'll just keep expecting more and more from you.

Activity 7: Rank Ordering
Purpose: This exercise provides students with an opportunity

to choose from among alternative courses of action or conditions. It allows them to work out the value conflicts that may often be involved.

Procedure: The teacher presents a question to the class orally. Three or four alternative choices are written on the chalkboard, and students are asked to rank their first, second, third, and fourth choices. Discussion of the choices then follows, the teacher asking five or six students how they ranked the responses and why. Other comments or questions are encouraged. The procedure may be repeated as often as is deemed necessary so that new insights can be revealed.

Following are a few sample questions and alternative choices:

1. What kind of job would you rather have?
   a. Where you know what's expected of you.
   b. Where you have to figure out what to do or how to do it.
   c. Where no one cares what you do.
   d. Where only you are affected if you don't do well.
2. If you could determine how much you got paid and there were no educational or training requirements involved, what would you rather be?
   a. A bus or truck driver
   b. A medical doctor
   c. A gardener
   d. A ski instructor
3. Which would it be most important for you to be?
   a. Rich
   b. Famous
   c. Powerful
   d. Helpful
4. If you had your choice of employers or supervisors in your first job, which type would you pick?
   a. Someone who is considerate and easygoing.
   b. Someone who won't tolerate any "goofing off."
   c. Someone who shows you how to get the job done.
5. What do you think would be the best reason for rewarding you with a promotion?
   a. Putting in more time than is required.
   b. Outproducing everyone in your group.
   c. Suggesting a highly successful innovation.
   d. Starting a highly successful employee morale program.

6. What do you think would be the most justifiable reason for getting fired?
   a. Refusing to follow an order that you think is stupid.
   b. Refusing to follow an order that you think will result in harm to yourself or others.
   c. Leading a protest against unfair hiring and promotion practices.
   d. Being consistently late for work.
7. What is the best way to get a job?
   a. Get your folks to call their friends for you.
   b. Answer the want ads.
   c. Go to the state employment service.
   d. Go to a private employment agency.
8. When you get information about a job opportunity, what is it best to do?
   a. Go to the firm immediately.
   b. Call on the telephone and make an appointment.
   c. Get one of your parents to call and make an appointment.
   d. Write a letter describing your qualifications and asking for an appointment.
9. If your foreman or supervisor reprimands you for sloppy work, which should you do?
   a. Just be quiet and take it.
   b. Explain that you had something else on your mind.
   c. Promise not to let it happen again.
   d. Explain that you aren't really any worse than anyone else.
10. In relationship to your father's or mother's career, which pattern should your own career follow?
    a. It ought to be at least as prestigious.
    b. It ought to be in an entirely different field.
    c. It shouldn't matter at all.

Exercises of this type are useful as an aid to students in clarifying and making explicit their internalized values. However, such exercises do not measure the intensity of those values; nor do they indicate ranking of those values under all possible conditions. Yet both intensity and ranking of values are important because most choices involve conflicts. We may desire many things, and eventually these desires may become excessive and mutually exclusive. We must make choices. And insofar as values predetermine our choices, it is the hierarchy and the intensity of these values that is important. For example, in occupational choice, salary may be the number-one consideration until a certain level is reached; then security or prestige or some other factor may slip into first place. Since these considerations are so significant, test instruments that examine either the strength of values or their relative intensity, or both, can be useful in values-clarification programs.

An example of one such test instrument is the Occupational Values Inventory developed by Impelletteri and Kapes (1971) at Pennsylvania State University. The test instrument is based upon empirical work that suggests the following as the most important values area related to occupational choice:

1. Interest and satisfaction
2. Advancement
3. Salary
4. Prestige
5. Personal goals
6. Preparation and ability
7. Security

Activity 8: Values Inventory

The Occupational Values Inventory tests the relative importance of values by requiring participants to establish rank among groups of three values that are related both within and across their areas. The instrument may be deficient in that its authors chose to leave out "altruism" as an area of consideration, and there is reason to think that the desire to be of service has been a value of rising interest among young persons in recent years. However, the Occupational Values Inventory is an example of a useful approach to values ranking. Participants are asked to examine thirty-four groups of three value statements each, and to indicate the values that they regard as "most important" and "least important." The following are from the inventory. The guiding statement concerns reasons for choosing a job. This exercise can be used for class discussion, student reports, or some of the statements may be assigned for a written report in the student's career plan workbook.

1. I can lose myself in this kind of work.
   There is a good possibility of elevation to top jobs.
   I can make a lot of money in this work.
2. This work is what I've planned for.
   I have the educational preparation for the job.

There is a labor shortage in this field.
3. I like the possible earnings from the job.
   People in this work are held in high regard.
   It has been my lifelong intention to get into this field.
4. There is an opportunity to do the things I've always wanted to do.
   I like working in a job environment that is attractive.
   The size of the paycheck interests me most.
5. There is honor associated with the work.
   I can be sure of a job even in hard times.
   I like the opportunities for advancement.
6. There is a lack of good people in this field.
   I can move upward quickly in this job.
   There is personal satisfaction for me in doing this work.
7. The work is stimulating to me.
   I can become financially well-off.
   Workers are wanted for this job.
8. There are higher positions that can be attained later.
   The job gives me a chance to be somebody.
   I am able to meet the requirements.
9. People on this job are admired by others.
   I am happy doing this work.
   The job is within my reach.
10. The job fits into my plan of life.
    There is a short supply of workers for this job.
    This career offers openings for better jobs in the future.
11. It's what I'd like to do as my lifework.
    This job can lead to better jobs.
    The work gives me a feeling of importance.
12. It's a job that I can give much attention to.
    There is a good beginning salary offered.
    I like the high regard that the job carries with it.
13. There is a need for workers in this area.
    The work brings with it a lot of prestige.
    I enjoy doing this kind of work.

Resources for Phase I, About the Student
Reading matter:
1. *Other Choices for Becoming a Woman*, and *Free to Choose: Decision Making for Young Men* (Delacorte, Dell Publishing Company, 245 East 47th Street, New York, NY 10017) by J. S. Mitchell. These books were designed to enable junior and senior high school students

to learn more about themselves. They are the first step in career education because they deal with Phase I — about the student. Students make good decisions if they can learn to think outside of stereotypes for girls and boys and to trust their own experiences of what they are like. Assign special chapters, or have students read different chapters and report to the class on what they have covered. There are specific chapters about career and educational choices, but the total concept of knowing more about oneself is the purpose of the two books.

2. *I Can Be Anything: Careers and Colleges for Young Women,* 1978, and *The Men's Career Book: Work and Life Planning for a New Age,* 1979 (Bantam Books, 666 Fifth Avenue, New York, NY 10019) by J. S. Mitchell. Assign the introduction of these books, which are written for high school students. The way young people are programmed to think about a career, the role of women or men in the world of work, making money, and equal partnership marriage are issues raised in these chapters that can help students learn more about themselves. The aim is to encourage students to think beyond the sex-role stereotypes as they make career decisions.

3. *The Work Book: A Guide to Skilled Jobs* (Bantam, 1978) by J. S. Mitchell. Assign the "Action Inventory" activity on page 11 to help your students find out more about their skills.

4. Ellen J. Wallach's chapter, "Life Career Skills: What Are You Going to Be When You Grow Up?" in J. S. Mitchell's *Be a Mother... And More: Career and Life Planning* (Bantam, 1980). This chapter provides a process for assessing personal skills.

5. *Decisions and Outcomes* and its companion publication, *Decisions and Outcomes: A Leader's Guide,* for high school students, by H. B. Gelatt, B. Varenhorst, R. Carey, G. T. Miller. Also *Deciding* and *Deciding: A Leader's Guide,* by H. B. Gelatt, B. Varenhorst, R. Carey (The College Board, 888 Seventh Avenue, New York, NY 10019) designed for junior high school students. These books are written as a course of study and can be used in helping students to learn how to make decisions.

6. *How to Decide: A Workbook for Women* (Avon Books, 959 Eighth Avenue, New York, NY 10019) by N. T. Scholz, J. S. Prince, G. P. Miller, an activities

workbook, designed especially for women, that can be used as a classroom aid to decision making.

Audio-Visual Material:

Anti-Defamation League of B'nai B'rith, Department M-1, 315 Lexington Avenue, New York, NY 10016, Telephone: 212-689-7400

"Eye of the Storm," 25 minutes, color, rental $20, purchase $325. Documents the Pygmalion effect.

"Island in America," 28 minutes, color, rental $17.50, purchase $250. Social, cultural, and economic life of Puerto Ricans

Association Films Inc., 866 Third Avenue, New York, NY 10022, Telephone: 212-935-4210

"The Future is Now" JC-101, 24 minutes, rental $9. Prejudice toward minority groups in areas of employment and education.

"North From Mexico: Exploration and Heritage" GP-101, 20 minutes, color, rental $16. Portrait of Chicanos finding their destiny through education and political action.

"The Princess in the Tower" JC-103, 22 minutes, color, rental $12.50. Musical film to aid in teaching healthy intergroup relations.

"16 in Webster Groves" CF-615, 47 minutes, rental $22.50. About growing up in Missouri. Has an excellent recommendation from Jim Loewen.

Everett/Edward Inc., P. O. Box 1060, Deland, FL 32720, Telephone: 904-734-7458

Audio cassettes:

5006 "Women & Employment," 5201 "Changing Roles of Males & Females," 5214 "The Prejudice of Parents"

William Greaves Productions, P. O. Box 315, Great Barrington, MA 01230

"In the Company of Men," "To Free Their Minds," "Whose Standard English"

Greenwood Press, 51 Riverside Avenue, Westport, CT 06880, Telephone: 203-226-3571

"Women Today: Options, Obstacles, Opportunities," 6 cassettes, $65; $11 each. Provokes wide-ranging discussion on female and male roles, responsibilities, and goals.

Guidance Associates, 757 Third Avenue, New York, NY 10017
"Jobs and Gender"

National Education Association, NEA Order Department, Academic Building, Saw Mill Road, West Haven, CT 06516, Telephone: 203-934-2669
"Sex Role Stereotyping," Multimedia kit

Syracuse University, Film Rental Center, 1455 East Colvin Street, Syracuse, NY 13210, Telephone: 315-479-6631
"Black Thumb" #1-10926, 7 minutes, color, rental $7.
"Your Self-Image" #1-9881, 8 minutes, color, rental $6.
"Marked for Failure" #3-5828, 60 minutes, rental $10.

Third World Newsreel, 26 West 20th Street, New York, NY 10011, Telephone: 212-243-2310
"Trick Bag," 30 minutes, black & white, rental $30. U.S. racism seen through the eyes of a Chicago youth.

About Work — Phase II

This phase describes activities that will lead the student to explore the world of work. Three major sources can provide information about work: 1. books and other media that describe work; 2. the work place, including professional associations, unions, agencies, businesses; and 3. the workers themselves. Students should be encouraged to read, write, talk, see, visit, and share information from these three sources. They must be critical as they explore these sources, making sure the information is up-to-date, nonsexist, nonracist, reliable, and provided by a person who has credibility.

The following activities explore any and all careers.

Activity 1: General Reading about Careers

1. *I Can Be Anything: Careers and Colleges for Young Women,* 1978 (Bantam Books, 666 Fifth Avenue, New York, NY 10019), by J. S. Mitchell.
2. *The Men's Career Book: Work and Life Planning for A*

New Age (Bantam, 1979), by J. S. Mitchell, a book dealing with careers that require two years of college through a Ph.D.

3. *The Work Book: A Guide to Skilled Jobs* (Bantam, 1978), by J. S. Mitchell. This is designed for the student seeking a career with high school training, or up to two years of post-secondary school training in trade, technical, and business jobs.

4. *Occupational Outlook Handbook*, published by the U.S. Bureau of Labor Statistics, and probably available in your guidance office, school library, or public library. The handbook describes more than 850 occupations.

I Can Be Anything, The Men's Career Book, and *The Work Book* are about work. They describe career possibilities. Have the students read through several careers in these books that sound good to them. If one career in a cluster interests the student, he or she should read several of the related occupations in that cluster. Using the clusters will help find new ideas. Sometimes young people tend to look only at business if they come from a business family whose relatives and family friends are mostly in business, or only in the military or government if most of their families are government workers. Have them start anew. On the other hand, sometimes because their family has told them "you ought to be" in business, or a dentist, or a new car dealer they may not like the idea. They reject it before seriously considering whether it's a good career or not. Have them explore career possibilities with themselves in mind, rather than the preconceptions of their family or friends. After they have researched some ideas they will have good reasons to look further, or to eliminate those possibilities.

Looking at all possibilities, then, have them find one or two or three careers that sound interesting enough to read and research further.

Activity 2: Acquiring Research Skills for Career Exploration

When students are reading the material, every basic question about careers may be qualified by a follow-up question, asking "What?"

Basic Career Questions	Follow-Up Questions
WHO does the work?	What are their PERSONAL QUALIFICATIONS?
WHAT do they do?	What are their EDUCATION OR TRAINING REQUIREMENTS?
	What do they DO? Major tasks they perform
	What do they KNOW? What they must understand to do the task
	What do they FEEL? What attitudes they need to be good workers
	What do they SPECIALIZE in?
WHY do they do it?	What SALARY do they make?
	What OPPORTUNITIES do they have for ADVANCEMENT?
WHEN do they do it?	What type of EMPLOYER do they work for?
WHERE do they do it?	What kind of CONDITIONS do they work in?
HOW do you get to do it?	What are the ALTERNATIVE WAYS TO ENTER this job?
	What is the SUPPLY AND DEMAND outlook for this job?

It is important that the students have a consistent list of questions to follow when seeking career information. They should complete this list for all the occupations they explore. As they find out additional information about one occupation, they should add that concept to their lists and go back and explore the concept for all the previous occupations they have investigated. Only in this manner will the students be able to fully evaluate all the alternatives. Otherwise, with only partial and inconsistent information about each, they would not be able to make a systematic decision.

The questions listed deal with general career matters. As your students begin to explore occupations they will be able to expand the list. You can develop a master list from the students' exercises and return these master lists to the students. This will truly expand their alternatives in each critical area.

The information that the students collect must prepare them to evaluate each occupation. They will be making an evaluation of the occupation from their frame of reference. Thus, the personal questions they ask must stem from what things they value as important. Encourage students to list at least one thing of personal importance to them in each of the information areas (qualifications, training, activities) and to ask a question about it.

It is important to emphasize to your students that their information gathering should be an ongoing process. As they get more information and more experience, they will view their worlds differently. Their needs will change. They will ask different questions, for they will be seeking different answers. So it is important that your students learn the skill of gathering information. They will use it often. They will not get by very well with one fixed list of questions.

Students generally have difficulty expanding a concept, or one of their values, into a list of questions they should ask. One way to help them identify the questions to ask is to have them first expand each single concept.

You expand a concept—such as "working conditions"—by applying each of the six basic questions to the concept. This will give you at least six questions to ask for each concept.

Question Development

BASIC QUESTIONS CONCEPT—working conditions

Who	do I work with, or for; or who works for me
What	is the temperature, noise level, danger, etc., associated with the work
Why	is the work done in this way and in this place, rather than another way or in another place
Where	would I go if there is an accident or an injury
When	will I have to be at work and when can I leave
How	will I have to dress, and is there any special equipment I will need

To the Student

Follow-up questions will help you get a basic understanding of what an occupation is all about. Some of these questions will give you information about WHAT THE CAREER WILL REQUIRE OF YOU, for example, the education and training requirements. Other questions will give you information about WHAT YOU WANT FROM THE CAREER, for example, the salary that it pays. There are many more questions you could add to these follow-up questions. The most important are ones that give you information about what you want from your career. Look at the questions being asked. Think about the things that are important to you in choosing a career. Make sure you have a question to ask that will give you information about the occupation in terms of what is important to you.

For example, you may want a good salary, but that is already on the list. You may want a challenging career that would let you *try new things*. You may want to *work closely with other people* on common tasks. You may also want a career that allows you to *plan* your work carefully and not be forced to rush into things just to meet deadlines.

Add these three personal questions to the follow-up questions list. Add your own personal follow-up questions to the list that you will use to get information from your reading. Think about things that are important to you in working. Fill in the blanks according to your own interests in the following activity.

Basic Questions   Follow-Up Questions

Basic Questions	Follow-Up Questions
WHO does the work?	What are their PERSONAL QUALIFICATIONS?
	What are the EDUCATION OR TRAINING REQUIREMENTS?
	PERSONAL: WHAT CHANCE WILL I HAVE TO WORK IN TEAMS WITH OTHERS?
	PERSONAL: _____
	PERSONAL: _____
WHAT do they do?	What ACTIVITIES do they perform?
	What do they DO? Major tasks they perform
	What do they KNOW? What they must understand to do the tasks
	What do they FEEL? What attitudes they need to be good workers

	What do they SPECIALIZE in?
WHY do they do it?	What SALARY do they make?
	What OPPORTUNITIES do they have for ADVANCEMENT?
	PERSONAL: WHAT CHANCE WILL I HAVE TO TRY NEW THINGS?
	PERSONAL: _____
	PERSONAL: _____
WHEN and WHERE do they do it?	What type of EMPLOYER do they work for?
	What kind of CONDITIONS do they work in?
HOW do you get to do it?	What are the ALTERNATIVE WAYS TO ENTER this job?
	What is the SUPPLY AND DEMAND outlook for this job?
	PERSONAL: WHAT CHANCE IS THERE TO PLAN MY OWN WORK SCHEDULE?
	PERSONAL: _____
	PERSONAL: _____

After your students have developed a master list of career information questions, you could have them develop a common format to use to write down their occupational information. This would enable you to start building a functional career information file. Each successive class could become responsible for updating and adding new occupations to the file. Or, a school file could be developed.

As some students gain career information, other students could practice their interviewing and information-seeking skills by using the first students as "experts" and questioning them. This would also show the first students where they are in need of more information.

Few students really understand the information they collect. They can rewrite it verbatim, but they don't always know what its value is for them. To help them understand the information they collect, you could have them go through one additional step of "personalizing" their information.

You personalize information by putting it in the following functional format.

If _____ (behavior)
then _____ (a job goal)
so that _____ (a human benefit)

For example, a computer operator must work with extreme

accuracy. If we were to personalize this information, it might look like this:

If I WORK WITH EXTREME ACCURACY AND MAKE NO MISTAKES then MY WORK WILL NOT HAVE TO BE CORRECTED BY OTHERS so that WE CAN GET THE JOB DONE MORE EFFICIENTLY AND MORE ECONOMICALLY
(or) I WILL GET A RAISE OR A PROMOTION FOR BEING SUCH A GOOD WORKER.

Have your students personalize all the information they collect. This will help both them and you make sure that they understand the information and how it relates them to the alternatives they are considering.

The students will find many important facts about the nature of the work involved in the careers they research. See the following example, where one student found out that he could become a computer programmer by going to a four-year college or a two-year college or by working his way through the ranks with on-the-job machine tabulation experience.

Basic Career Questions	**Computer Programmer**	
WHO does the work?	PERSONAL QUALIFICATIONS	Work with extreme accuracy; patience; persistence; ingenuity; imagination; logical thinking.
	EDUCATION AND TRAINING	4-year college degree for science and engineering; 2-year college degree for specialty areas in business records plus on-the-job training experience.
	PERSONAL (TEAMWORK)	Work closely with other programmers and specialists on large projects.

WHAT do they do?	ACTIVITIES	Prepare computer instructions; debug programs.
	KNOWLEDGE	Know how to analyze problems.
	ATTITUDE	Willing to discipline themselves to spend long hours paying great attention to detail.
WHY do they do it?	SALARY	$8,000 to $17,000; $10,000 average.
	OPPORTUNITIES FOR ADVANCEMENT	Very good for skilled programmers; the options are positions as supervisors and managers of computer department, or systems analysts.
	PERSONAL (CHALLENGING)	Computer settings focusing on application-programming constantly demand new ways to meet objectives.
WHEN and WHERE do they do it?	WHERE EMPLOYED	Primarily in large business organizations and government agencies.
	WORKING CONDITIONS	Modern, well-lighted, air-conditioned offices; 40-hour work week; usually day work with some programmers working other shifts in special problems.
HOW do they do it?	ALTERNATIVE WAYS TO ENTER	Many computer companies and private training companies will train high school graduates in the necessary skills; technical and vocational schools are beginning to offer training programs.
	SUPPLY AND DEMAND	Good job outlook as computers get wider acceptance and usage in more industries, especially for 2-year business graduates.

PERSONAL (PLANNING)	Planning time may often exceed application time.

Using the master sheets of basic career questions with personal questions to follow up, have each student select a first, second, and third career alternative. Students can look in depth at all of the alternatives as they research careers through reading. Have the students enter their research results in their career plan workbook.

Basic Career Questions

WHO does the work?   PERSONAL
                     QUALIFICATIONS _____
                     _____
                     _____

                     EDUCATION AND
                        TRAINING _____
                     PERSONAL _____
                     PERSONAL _____
WHAT do they do?   ACTIVITIES _____
                     _____

                     KNOWLEDGE _____
                     ATTITUDE _____
                     AREAS OF
                        SPECIALIZATION _____

                     PERSONAL _____
                     PERSONAL _____
WHY do they do it?   SALARY_____
                     OPPORTUNITIES FOR
                        ADVANCEMENT _____

                     PERSONAL _____
                     PERSONAL _____
WHEN and WHERE   WHERE EMPLOYED _____
do they do it?   _____
                     WORKING CONDITIONS _____

                     PERSONAL _____
                     PERSONAL _____
HOW do they do it?   ALTERNATIVE WAYS
                        TO ENTER _____
                     _____

SUPPLY AND
    DEMAND _____
PERSONAL _____
PERSONAL _____

Activity 3: Reading About People on the Job

There are many interesting articles and books about people who have careers, or about the jobs themselves. Beware of articles that glamorize the person's life! Be sure to notice whether the information is up-to-date. Your library card catalog is a good place to locate books, as is the subject index to *Books in Print*. *The Reader's Guide to Periodical Literature* locates magazine articles for you or for your students. Start with *Working* by Studs Terkel (Avon). It's a book about people who describe what they do all day and how they feel about what they do. All kinds of workers from skycap and piano tuner to TV executive and spot-welder tell their working story.

Also have them read *Pink Collar Workers* by Louise Kapp Howe (Avon), which describes women in their work as beauticians, sales workers, waitresses, office workers, and homemakers.

Activity 4: Reading Trade Magazines

If you want to help your students get the inside story of what people already in a particular career are reading, thinking about, and actually doing, have them read the relevant trade magazine. By reading the *Wall Street Journal, Variety,* and *Veterinary Economics* they will find out what the financial, theater, and vet people are really about. It's not academic theory but the *business* of the job that they will find in the trade magazines. This reading also provides excellent preparation for a job interview. Nothing will impress a book publisher more than a student's ability to rattle off the business after reading about it in the *Publishers Weekly*, for example. Physicians will be similarly impressed if students quote from the *New England Journal of Medicine*, or bankers if they have the latest from the *American Banker*, or urban planners if students are aware of what's in *City*. If the school library doesn't have the relevant trade magazines, check the community library, or a college library. A list of trade magazines in career clusters that require at least two years of college follows:

ART, DESIGN, AND COMMUNICATION CAREERS

Performing Arts:
 Actor: *Variety*
 Dancer: *Dance Magazine, Dance News*
 Musician: *Billboard, Creem, Rolling Stone*

Design:
 Architect: *Architectural Record*
 Commercial artist: *Art in America, The Illustrator Magazine*
 Industrial designer: *Industrial Design*
 Interior designer: *Interiors*
 Landscape architect: *Landscape Architecture*
 Photographer: *Popular Photography*

Communications:
 Linguist: *Quinto Lingo*
 Museum: *Museum News*
 Radio and television employee: *Broadcasting*
 Writer: *Journal of Technical Writing and Communications, Editor & Publisher—the Fourth Estate, Publishers Weekly*

BUSINESS, SALES, AND OFFICE CAREERS

 Accountant: *Journal of Accountancy*
 Actuary: *Risk Management*
 Advertising: *Advertising Age*
 Automobile salesperson: *Automobile News*
 Bank officer: *American Banker*
 Business executive: *Fortune, Business Management, MBA*
 City manager: *Nation's Cities*
 City planner: *City*
 Computer programmer: *Computers and People*
 Credit manager: *Credit and Financial Management*
 Hotel-motel-restaurant manager: *Nation's Restaurant News, Hotel and Motel Management*
 Industrial traffic manager: *Traffic Management*
 Lawyer: *Trial*
 Insurance broker: *The Insurance Salesman*
 Manufacturers' salesperson: *The American Salesman*
 Market researcher: *Marketing News*
 Merchandise manager: *Marketing Times, Women's Wear Daily*
 Personnel and labor relations administrator: *Personnel Administrator*
 Public relations officer: *Public Relations Quarterly*
 Purchasing agent: *Purchasing*

Real estate broker: *Appraisal Journal*
Secretary: *Today's Secretary*
Stockbroker: *Wall Street Journal*
Systems analyst: *Computerworld*
Travel agent: *Travel Trade*

EDUCATION CAREERS

Child-care worker: *Day Care and Early Education*
College professor: *AAUP Bulletin*
Guidance counselor: *Guidepost*
High school teacher: *Today's Education*
Librarian: *Top of the News, Library Journal*
Museum worker: *Museum News*
School administrator: *Nation's Schools*

GOVERNMENT CAREERS

Civil servant: *Civil Service Journal*
Military: *Army Times, Air Force Times, Navy Times, Marine Corps Gazette, Coast Guard Engineer's Digest*

HEALTH CAREERS

Chiropractor: *Today's Chiropractic*
Dental Hygienist: *Dental Hygiene*
Dentist: *ADA News*
Doctor: *New England Journal of Medicine*
Health service administrator: *Hospitals*
Medical record administrator: *Medical Record News*
Nurse: *RN*
Optometrist: *Optometric Management*
Osteopath: *The Osteopathic Physician*
Pharmacist: *American Druggist*
Podiatrist: *American Podiatry Association Journal*
Veterinarian: *Veterinary Economics*

SCIENTIFIC AND TECHNICAL CAREERS

Astronomer: *Weatherwise or Meteorologist*
Biologist: *American Naturalist*
Chemist: *Chemical Technology*
Conservationist: *Forest Industries*
Ecologist: *Rocks and Minerals*
Engineer: *Chemical Engineering, Civil Engineering, Electronics, Engineering News-Record, Mechanical Engineering*
Environmental scientist: *Sea Frontiers, National Wildlife*

Food scientist: *Quick Frozen Foods International*
Mathematician: *Mathematics Magazine*
Physicist: *Physics Today*

SERVICES AND SOCIAL SERVICES CAREERS

Extension service worker: *Extension Service Review*
Funeral director and embalmer: *The Director*
Home economist: *What's New in Home Economics?*
Law enforcement: *National Sheriff*
Recreation worker: *Recreation Management*
Rehabilitation counselor: *Social and Rehabilitation Record*
Religious worker: *Christian Century, Commentary, Commonwealth*
Social worker: *Social Work*

SOCIAL SCIENCES CAREERS

Anthropologist: *Anthropology Newsletter*
Economist: *American Economic Review*
Geographer: *Annals*
Historian: *American Heritage*
Political scientist: *Political Science Quarterly*
Psychologist: *Behavioral Science*
Sociologist: *Society*

TRANSPORTATION CAREERS

Airline pilot: *Flying*
Air traffic controller: *Journal of Air Traffic Control*
Flight attendant: *Passenger & In-flight Service*
Merchant marine officer: *Seaway Review*

Activity 5: Reading the Yellow Pages

The Yellow Pages of the telephone book (either a local directory or one from a major city, which will be available in the library) can give your students an idea of what sources of employment exist in a certain field. They can make a directory of local resources. For example, a directory of music businesses would include:

Background music
Recording studios
Music publishers
Record companies

Sheet music
Musical instrument sales/rental
Musical instrument manufacturers
Radio stations
Talent agencies
Concert promoters

Activity 6: Reading the Want Ads

Classified ("want") advertisement sections of Sunday newspapers can tell students something about the job market. Have them see what kinds of jobs are available in their field of interest. Also look for jobs in other fields that require some of the skills from their field.

Examples:

a. Sales jobs that require fluency in a foreign language.

b. Personnel jobs calling for excellent writing skills.

Students can also call the local state employment office (Division of Employment Security) to ask if any jobs are available in their field of interest.

Activity 7: Writing to Professional Associations

Have the students write to the professional associations and unions listed at the end of each job description in the books indicated under Activity 1, page 42, and request pamphlets that contain information about careers and colleges. Have them check the publication date of all written sources because those produced even as recently as 1975 may contain inaccurate information, especially about the job outlook. You can start a central file of career information for your classroom, and especially for your own subject matter or level. Be aware that most career pamphlets are sexist and racist, even though they are designed for high school students.

Activity 8: Writing for Recommended Readings

Write to the publishers cited under "Recommended Readings" in Mitchell's books listed under Activity 1 (see page 42). Include these booklets and articles in your classroom career information file.

Activity 9: Make a Career-Talk List

Almost every field has its own vocabulary. Usually the words are technical, but in fields such as jazz, knowing the slang vocabulary is necessary for communicating. Compiling a mini-dictionary of words related to a particular field will increase students' knowledge about work in that field.

Activity 10: Interviewing Workers

Talking to people who work in careers that interest the student is a great way to learn. Most people enjoy talking about themselves if the interview does not take more than half an hour. But, to be sure to get interesting and helpful information, prepare the students with a list of questions to take with them.

Some sample questions for students to ask are:

a. What is your job title?
b. What tasks do you spend most of your time doing for your job?
c. What is the educational background required for your job?
d. What are the main skills or competencies you need for your job?
e. What are the main personality traits required?
f. Why did you decide to become a _____?
g. What are some advantages of your job?
h. What are some disadvantages of your job?
i. What job can you move to that has more responsibility and pay?
j. Is there much competition for a job like yours?
k. Are you paid on a salary or a free-lance basis? How does your income compare with that of people who do similar work in other parts of the country? What are the salary ranges and how do you get increases in salary? (But *not* "How much do you earn?")

The student may want to team with a classmate to conduct the interview. Students with a broad interest in a field may learn more by interviewing several people with different jobs in one field.

Examples:

a.   In a television station, they can talk to a news announcer, a sound engineer, a camera person, a continuity writer, a business manager.

b.   In the teaching field they could talk to a kindergarten teacher, a junior high teacher, an industrial arts teacher, an athletic coach, a number of college professors in different subjects, a superintendent, and so on.

c.   In a hospital, they could talk to a hospital administrator, a lab technician, a physician, a dietitian, and a physician's assistant.

Students may find that their families can help put them in touch with others who are already in the career they are thinking about. If the student wants to sell securities he should consult a stockbroker about what it's like to be in this field. How much of the job is really rewarding and how much is distasteful? Have the students listen to everything they hear from others as it relates to them, because they are the ones who will be doing the selling—enjoying the hustle and competition, or getting an ulcer until they finally make the sale.

Students will find that, in addition to their families, many teachers are good sources for finding people in careers that they are ready to research. Clergy, youth group leaders, and many people in the community including the alumni from the same school are all people who want to help young people with career development. Some of them already have specific programs in this direction while others are looking for ways to help. Have the students ask them if they know a forester, a computer systems analyst, or a foreign service officer who could be interviewed as an aid to career research. Students don't have to wait until they are choosing a college major or hunting for a job to begin interviews. The more experience they have talking with people in work that interests them, the more background they will have for their decisions ahead. The interview experience will be good training for future interviews, but also it will have value right now as students learn more about work and the ways that it will fit into their life.

Students are in a good position for exploring. They have a positive image and cannot be considered a competitive threat to those already holding jobs—so have them make the most of their student status to reach out to learn about careers from the people doing well in them.

After they have the names of people to interview have them call and express their desire to talk to someone who knows about the job. They should say that they would like a specific amount of time for the interview, so that the workers won't think the students will keep them too long from their work. As soon as the student gets home, a short thank-you note to the interviewee for both time granted and sharing of work information is a necessary follow-up.

Activity 11: Inviting Speakers to Your Classroom

Invite speakers to your classroom to discuss their work. It is interesting to have a panel of three or four speakers who work in the same field, but in different settings.

For example:

a. An economist who teaches on the college level, an economist who works for the state government, and an economist who works for a profit-making business.

b. An editor of a weekly newspaper, a department editor for a daily newspaper, and an editor of a magazine published locally.

Another interesting panel is one composed of people who work in the same setting but have different jobs (like the television station, hospital, and teacher examples in Activity 10). Another possibility is combining people who work in the same field, but including one who works full-time, one who works part-time, and one who carries out volunteer activities.

It's a good idea to tell your speaker or panel members before they arrive the topics they should discuss. Questions similar to the ones used in interviews are helpful.

Without doubt, one of the best ways to provide students with current and realistic occupational information is through talking with people in the field. Not only do practitioners give facts about the work they do, but they also breathe life into this information; they generate a special personal quality concerning their work with which secondary school students can readily identify. Teachers must watch out, however, for one major pitfall in this kind of learning experience: students could be interested or uninterested in a job in direct proportion to whether they like or dislike the person describing it. Although certain kinds of people are sometimes drawn to certain kinds of jobs, teachers should encourage students to divorce the personality of the worker interviewed from the work she does.

Career specialists can reinforce the work of teachers who are attempting to show the practical application of the subjects they teach, or they may take part in a general career exploration program in the school. Programs such as shadowing and independent study that occur away from school need the talents of community specialists.

Methods for identifying people in the community include:

a. Examining the data already accumulated on each student and his family
b. Asking teachers to poll students concerning the work roles of family members
c. Mailing a general letter or brochure to all homes—this is especially appropriate for a small community or neighborhood
d. Asking teachers to name people they know
e. Contacting firms and individuals that have hired students and graduates, or that have provided field trips or shadowing experiences
f. Checking the Yellow Pages

Check the wide variety of existing community agencies and organizations found in almost every community which are already actively involved in helping young people in career awareness, career exploration, and career decision making. Examples of such agencies and organizations include:

Chamber of Commerce
Local service clubs (Rotary, Lions, Kiwanis)
American Legion and Legion Auxiliary
Exploring Program, Scouting, USA
Girl Scouts of America
Junior Achievement
Local labor union councils
Local apprenticeship councils
Local CETA operations
Local Council of Churches
YWCA
YMCA
National Alliance of Businessmen
Women's American ORT
Council of Business and professional women's clubs

Grange
National Urban Coalition
National Association for the Advancement of Colored
    People
National Organization for Women

Contact newspaper sources, professional associations, service groups, and unions.

In looking for community resources, consider young workers especially, because students can identify with them and their experiences and because their occupational information is likely to be current.

When the identification process is underway, you will need specific information in order to determine which community members are willing to help in career exploration and how best to use their talents and knowledge. The following sample questionnaire incorporates this kind of information.

Community Practitioners

Name: _____ Date: _____

Telephone: _____ Job title: _____

Product or service provided: _____
_____

What kinds of specific activities do you do? _____
_____
_____
_____

Please check any of the following subjects used in your work:
Language arts: ____Reading ____Writing ____Speaking
____Foreign languages ____Science ____Mathematics
____Music ____Industrial arts ____Visual arts
____History ____Social sciences (economics, sociology)
____Other _____
Name and address of place where work performed: _____
_____
_____

Do you have any hobbies related to your work? _____
_____

Would you be willing to come to school at a convenient time to discuss your work and interests with students?
                    ____Yes ____No ____Maybe

Would you be willing to have a student or group of students visit you at work?

_____ Yes _____ No _____ Maybe

Would you be willing to provide an occupational learning experience (e.g., internship, apprenticeship, work-study) to an interested student?

_____ Yes _____ No _____ Maybe

Community resource people are most effective when they have suggestions from the school on which to base a presentation. The in-school visit will mean more to students if they participate in developing questions that they want most to be answered. The following questions are suggested for stimulating the imaginations of both the resource people and the students.

Suggested Questions for Community Practitioners

Qualifications and Job Duties

a. What abilities do you need to *do* the job?
b. What do you do in an ordinary day? week?
c. With what other people do you come in contact and for what reasons?
d. What kind of education or special training was necessary to acquire the job? Where is this available? How long does it take to complete? How much does it cost?
e. What secondary school courses are useful in performing your work?
f. Do you have to belong to a union or a professional association?
g. Do you need special licensing or certification?
h. Do you need special tools or clothing?
i. Are there any physical conditions that could disqualify an applicant for the work (e.g., visual or hearing impairment)?

Career Opportunities

a. How did you hear about the job opening or the fact that such a job existed?
b. Did you choose the job or did it just happen?
c. What are the possibilities for advancement? for increased income? for job security?
d. What technological or societal trends may affect your job?
e. Do you need to take courses or lessons to improve your ability or salary?

f. What else could you be doing with your skills and knowledge?
g. Do you consider this job temporary or is it permanent?
h. Are there job opportunities in this field throughout the United States?
i. Are there summer or part-time openings in your work?
j. Are there other settings where your work is done?
k. Are there good opportunities for women and minority groups in this field in positions of responsibility?

Working Conditions

a. How many hours a day (week) do you spend working? at the job location? at home?
b. Do you consider the pay good? adequate? poor? Is this usual? Are there any bonuses? overtime pay? fringe benefits? paid vacations?
c. Do you do any strenuous physical work?
d. Do you have any especially busy seasons?
e. Do you work alone? with other people present?
f. Are you part of a team?
g. Do you help people? In what way?
h. Do you work mainly with ideas? with things?
i. Do you work indoors?
j. Do you make a lot of decisions? What kind?
k. Do you do the same kind of work repeatedly?
l. Does your job require much travel?
m. Are you able to choose *how* your work is done?
n. Do you meet interesting people as part of your work?
o. Do you have to be "nice" to other people?
p. What does your work place look like?

Personal Considerations

a. Do you think your job is important?
b. In what way do you find the job different from your expectations of it?
c. What made you decide to enter this field?
d. Did anyone influence your choice?
e. What do you like best about your work? least?
f. What do you find frustrating? boring? interesting?
g. If you didn't have to work for a living, would you continue to do this work?
h. What was your greatest accomplishment related to your work?

i. What advice would you give to students who are considering this kind of work?

Faculty and Staff Members as Career Information Resources

The school itself can be a rich source for obtaining occupational information. Teachers and administrators may have had other jobs before they worked in education, or they may be involved in such jobs during their time away from school. Many also have avocational pursuits in these fields. One way to tap their backgrounds is to develop a resource card file for use on career days, in panel presentations, and individual interviews.

At the beginning of the academic year, the counselor might ask all faculty and staff members to complete cards containing the following questions:

Name: _____ Date: _____
Have you ever had a job other than public school teaching in any of the following fields?

____ Sciences	____ Visual arts
____ Dance	____ Writing
____ Music	____ Mathematics
____ Theater and media	____ Technology
____ Foreign languages	____ Museum work
____ History	____ Religion
____ Law	____ Social sciences

What specifically did you do?
Do you have any hobbies that are related to the above fields? Would you be willing to talk to students about these experiences?

Activity 12: Shadow Day

Using the community resources you have developed, organize a "shadow day" for each of your class members. Arrange for each student to spend the workday with someone in the community who is in a career related to your curriculum. Shadow day will provide students with learning experiences that will aid them in making career decisions; it will help them to develop an appreciation for the skills, responsibilities, and values of working people; and to provide closer ties between the school and the community, thus making their classwork more relevant.

Activity 13: Looking at Audio-Visual Materials

Many films, filmstrips, cassettes, and other audio-visuals have been made to help students explore careers. There are also others produced for a different purpose that contain some career information. Here are some good audio-visual materials to start with:

Butterick Publishing, P. O. Box 1945, Altoona, PA 16603, Telephone: 814-943-5281 (Attention: Susan Clark)
  "American Woman: New Opportunties"
  "American Man: New Opportunties"

Dibie-Dash Productions, Inc., 4949 Hollywood Boulevard (Suite 208), Hollywood, CA 90027, Telephone: 213-663-1915
  "A Black Experience," 25 minutes, color, purchase $280. Traces the folklore of the American Negro from the days of slavery through the present.
  "They Beat the Odds," 22 minutes, color, purchase $230. Lives of several successful black professionals.

Educational Activities, Inc., 1937 North Grand Avenue, Baldwin, NY, Telephone: 516-BA3-4666
  "Career Awareness II"
  Filmstrip/cassette

Time/Life Multimedia Distribution Center, 100 Eisenhower Drive, Paramus, NJ 07652, Telephone: 201-843-4545
  "51 Percent" Videotape, rental $25. Women in business, men and women discussing how roles have changed.

Activity 14: Visiting the Work Place

Visits to the places where people work are fun and informative. Arrange for small groups or the whole class to go. Alert the people that the students will be asking them questions about their *jobs*. It's interesting for students to jot down before they visit a product designer's office, for example, what they expect the person's job to be like; after the visit they can talk with their classmates about whether everyone's expectations turned out to be realistic.

Activity 15: Peer Sharing

Have the students share their newly acquired information with the class by giving an oral report. They might choose to report on all the questions that were answered in one interview, or to focus on one question—such as skills that may be needed in the future because of technological change—that they have learned about from several sources.

Share with the students information and ideas about jobs or volunteer work you have had.

Activity 16: Charting Job Information

Another way for classmates to share information is to make posters or information sheets that chart job information. The class will probably need one poster for each job explored. The posters might include the following information:

Job title
Skills and competencies needed
Skills and competencies that may be needed in the future
Educational requirements
Special talents needed
Special personality characteristics needed
Geographic location
Settings
Ways of acquiring jobs
Career ladders
Average income for your locality
Average income for New York or elsewhere
Nature of income
Need for additional income
Job outlook
Advantages
Disadvantages
Moral conflicts
Resource: Career Education Wall Charts, $2 each; a set of 25
  for $29.95; Garrett Park Press, Garrett Park, MD 20766

Activity 17: Occupational Card Sorting

Purpose: This activity expands students' knowledge about the range of possible occupations. In choosing among them, students begin to examine their personal interests and aptitudes as they relate to work roles. Because the job titles specified are only a representative sample of many hundreds, the teacher may desire to add others that are important to a particular student population.

Procedures: One method of conducting the occupational card sort requires the teacher or students to compile a list of job titles and to duplicate and cut this into job cards. When the materials are prepared, each student should:

1. receive two or three sets of cards—one of health jobs, one of business jobs, or any cluster that fits your subject matter. These are kept separate from each other. For identification purposes, each card has a cluster initial in the upper right-hand corner (e.g., H for health, B for business, S for science);
2. divide the health cards into three piles according to jobs that students might *like* to do, those they are indifferent to, and those they would not like to do;
3. rank order those in the "like to do" pile and list the titles of the top ten (if there are that many);
4. this time divide the job title cards into three new piles according to whether students have the *aptitude* to do the job in question, do not know if they could do it, or do not think they have the aptitude to do it;
5. rank order the job titles in the "aptitude" pile and write the top ten titles (if there are that many) on the same paper as the other top ten;
6. note at the bottom of this paper any job titles that appear in both lists;
7. follow the same steps in using the business or other job title clusters.

Activity 18: Fringe Benefits

Assign a group of students to call, talk with, or correspond with a large national company, a large local company, a small local business, and someone who is self-employed. Inquire about fringe benefits offered employees. Construct a chart of the benefits offered.

The class as a whole should first discuss what fringe benefits (such as health or life insurance plans, educational aids, pension plans, vacations, paid holidays, merchandise discounts, and bonus payments) they wish to inquire about. The economic impact of these benefits both for the employer and the employee should be considered.

If businesses are reluctant to give the students information, have them talk with their parents about the benefits offered on their jobs.

Educational Pathways — Phase III

There are many educational pathways for career preparation. These include extracurricular activities, summer programs, after-school jobs, training in specialized high schools, courses in high schools, community colleges, technical colleges, trade and business schools, traditional colleges, nontraditional colleges, motherhood, stopout programs, work-study plans and programs, apprenticeships, military training, correspondence study, and on-the-job training.

The Director of U. S. Career Education, Dr. Hoyt, stresses that educators must no longer assume that the more years one spends in school, the better equipped one is for work. The optimum kind and amount of education required as preparation for work will vary widely from career to career. A college degree is no longer the best and surest route to occupational success, and it is important that this be understood by both students and their parents. While the *multiple* educational goals of college education may well be increasing in importance, the pure *economic* advantage of the college degree is on the decline. It is important that, in terms of the goal of education as preparation for work, various forms of postsecondary education—including work experience outside the structure of formal education—be viewed as differing in *kind* rather than in intrinsic *worth*. Further, the educational goals of the institution should bear some direct relationship to the student's educational goals. To the extent that education as preparation for work represents a goal important to the student, the educational institution has a responsibility to state clearly the importance *it* attaches to that goal and the ways in which it seeks to meet it. Career education efforts are strongly oriented toward helping both students and educational institutions understand and act upon the relative importance that the goal of education as preparation for work holds both for the student and for the institution.

Check the resources at the end of this chapter for specialized books concerning educational pathways. Especially see *What's Where: The Official Guide to College Majors* (Avon, 1979), and "Where Can I Get the Skills?" in *The Work Book: A Guide to Skilled Jobs* (Bantam, 1978).

Choosing a college major, choosing technical or business training, and choosing work experiences are educational pathways or directions toward career decisions. In addition to going to college, or in addition to the classroom experience are the actual work experiences where students can try their ideas from school in a work situation.

When you cover educational pathways with your students, consider also:

Extracurricular Activities

For the student who has made a tentative choice to pursue a career, participation in related extracurricular activities can be crucial. Especially in performance fields (dance, athletics, music, theater, the media, industrial arts, commercial and distributive education) and in art and writing careers, extracurricular activities—both in junior and senior high— may be the key to admission in specialized educational programs and later the key to obtaining a job. Besides your own school activity, or others offered in your school, students should be encouraged to look into community resources as well as traditional school clubs and programs. In particular, the advanced or highly motivated student will benefit from volunteer involvement with cultural institutions, individual professionals, health and recreation programs, businesses, newspapers, and television stations.

Work Experience

Once students get an idea that makes sense for them they can use their summer vacation, after-school time, and weekends for a trial of their idea. Whether it's paid or volunteer work, encourage your students to work on construction if they are interested in the building business, or in a hospital if they are interested in a health career, with a children's group in a day camp or child-care center if they are interested in education, in a bookstore or publishing house if the book business interests them. Have them try a summer job in a bank or real estate office if finance is their interest.

Even though the kind of work they can get is the lowest level in that field—and reserved for beginners—the menial becomes meaningful if students apply what they learn to their own career development. If they are doing a repetitious job that takes no thinking, urge them to look around at the whole system and notice what the next jobs are for people who have permanent jobs in the place, or who are there for their second summer, or who have had promotions. Who is their immediate boss, and who is the next boss? Does that job look interesting? A summer job in a real-estate office may consist of painting front doors on homes to be sold. But they can learn to look around and see the hours of the other sales people, listen to the kinds of questions clients ask, listen to the answers, notice which sales people are making the most money, which are putting in the most time, which are living a life they would like to live.

Summer Programs

School extracurricular activities can be augmented by jobs, community programs, or special training in the summers or after school. Community recreation departments and other agencies often hire teenagers in the summer. This is a good time for students to try things that are both related or seemingly completely unrelated to their school year. It's especially a good time to discover that something "works" or "doesn't work" for them. They can use their summer experiences for one more input into their decision making toward a career. Have your students read "Summer Time Is Discovery Time" in Mitchell's *Free to Choose: Decision Making for Young Men* (Delacorte, Dell) or *Other Choices for Becoming a Woman* (Delacorte, Dell) to learn ideas for camping, hiking, or biking; study or the arts; volunteer or paid work.

Specialized High Schools

Metropolitan area public schools are increasingly establishing specialized schools in the performing, creative, and visual arts, humanities, math, and science. There are regional technical public schools in every part of the country. These schools may offer academic courses in addition to special courses, or may require that students spend part of the school day at a "home" high school for academics and the remainder at the specialized school.

Students must audition or be tested for admission to many specialized public high schools. Upon admission they work with faculty who are proficient as teachers and are usually also specialized in the same field of interest. Check with the guidance department in your school to help your students learn their choices for specialized public schools in your local area.

High School Curriculum

Assign to your students "Curriculum Choices" in Mitchell's *Other Choices for Becoming a Woman* and *Free to Choose* for ideas about course selection. Help students learn the benefits of your particular subject for a career and the relevance of taking your course while in high school for related careers.

Motherhood

If young women are to take career education seriously, it's imperative for them to see motherhood as part of it. Young women expect to be mothers. Not until they understand that mothers learn transferable skills such as problem-identification, problem-solving and time-management every time they tend a crying baby—will they begin to see all of their life in terms of career development.

Stopouts

Another work alternative, besides summer and after-school work, is an internship or voluntary program for an academic year or summer in place of going to college. An internship is a supervised work experience where students can learn about a career or field of interest. Usually they are not paid, but often they can earn credits. Many students stop out of school for a year after high school or after their first year of college to test a career idea. A basic guide for internships during the academic years is *Stopout! Working Ways to Learn* (Avon, 1979), by J. S. Mitchell. And for summer internships, read the *National Directory of Summer Internships for Undergraduate College Students* (Bryn Mawr and Haverford College, every year), by M. E. Updike and M. E. Rivera. The time students use to explore jobs pays off in experience and learning about themselves as well as the money or credits they can earn.

Stopouts have become so popular that up to half of the students at places like Harvard, Swarthmore, and Stanford are stopping out for work experience. A Princeton junior took a job as a hospital orderly for ten months; he came back convinced that medicine was his vocation. Even though a medical orderly is at the other end of the hospital hierarchy from a doctor, the stopout enabled him to learn about medicine as a system, see the different jobs within it, and be sure about the one he was after. Another student, Doris Sawyer, from the University of California, stopped out of college twice to see what the world of work was like. Her second stopout included a job in a real-estate agency, where she learned about business on her own. When she returned to college it was with a practical sense of how to go about the career she had chosen: real-estate sales. What does she say she learned? "I learned in business that if you want something, you've got to go for it."

Advising Students

The major difficulty in advising students about educational pathways is that they often have had little opportunity to test their aptitudes in these areas. It is usually best to recommend the broadest choice of courses within social studies, technical programs, language arts, business, mathematics, science, and foreign languages. Because definite occupational commitments are often not made by students until well into their college years, or even later, their high school programs should include as many in-depth courses as they can handle well. If possible they should avoid specializing in high school. The earlier they make educational decisions, the more they transfer and drop out of their specialized programs. If students focus on finding out about themselves, assessing their skills, getting in tune with their values and interests as they change, and keeping their career options open for new directions—they can't go wrong!

Resources for Educational Pathways

1. For the high school student who is going to college:
    What's Where: The Official Guide to College Majors, Avon
    The College Handbook, The College Board
    Comparative Guide to American Colleges, Harper and Row
    Guide to Alternative Colleges and Universities, Beacon Press
    Hawes' Comprehensive Guide to Colleges, New American Library
    Meeting College Costs, The College Board
    This Way Out: A Guide to Alternatives to Traditional College Education, Dutton

2. For the high school student who is going into trade, technical or business careers:
    The Work Book: A Guide to Skilled Jobs, Bantam
    By Hand: A Guide to Schools and a Career in Crafts, Dutton
    Getting Skilled: A Guide to Private Trade and Technical Schools, Dutton

3. For the high school student who wants to stop out of school for a year before continuing his or her college education:
    Stopout! Working Ways to Learn, Avon

4. For the female high school student:
    Other Choices for Becoming a Woman, Delacorte, Dell
    I Can Be Anything: Careers and Colleges for Young Women, Bantam
    Be a Mother...And More: Career and Life Planning, Bantam

5. For the nonwhite high school student:
    Directory of Special Programs for Minority Group Members: Career Information Services, Employ-

ment Skills Banks, Financial Aid Sources, Garrett Park Press (Garrett Park, MD 20766)
Financial Aid for Minority Students, Garrett Park Press

6. For the disabled high school student:
   The College Guide for Students with Disabilities, Abt Associates (55 Wheeler Street, Cambridge, MA 02138)
   A Guide to College and Career Programs for Deaf Students, National Technical Institute for the Deaf (1 Lomb Memorial Drive, Rochester, NY 14623)

7. For the gifted and talented high school student:
   From the Council for Exceptional Children (1920 Association Drive, Reston, VA 22091): 1. *Providing Programs for the Gifted and Talented—A Handbook* ($6.45). 2. *Gifted and Talented: Developing Elementary and Secondary School Programs* ($3.00).

INTEGRATING STRATEGIES FOR THE CLASSROOM

Integrating or connecting or blending the process of career exploration with the process of teaching the "ir" verbs in French, or instrumentation in music, or rhyme schemes in English, or the keyboard in typing calls for much more imagination from you than does a six-week set-aside for "Now we're going to talk about careers." The transition from subject matter to exploring careers related to that subject may seem artificial when it occurs outside the context of answering students' specific questions.

This transition can, however, take place smoothly, and in most situations, rationally. Even when students show no interest in their future beyond high school or college or when the subject matter seems to offer only artificial integration (an example for both problems may be a junior high marching band), there are strategies to introduce at least the beginnings of career exploration.

In the case of the junior high marching band, the band director could start out a rehearsal by saying, "How did the sheet music for this piece get here?" That simple question can lead to a discussion of all kinds of careers related to music and business, and for interested students to a discussion of what kind of career might evolve from being a member of a junior high marching band. By spending no more than twenty minutes like this in the whole year, the band director can get a transition from what a student is doing to a concept of possible careers.

Suggestions for providing the transition between the regular course content and the career exploration material are listed later in this chapter. These transitions, or integrating strategies, may be in the form of a classroom activity or a specific discussion topic or a general relationship. You may choose to cover only one job group with the whole class, letting highly motivated students conduct individual or small group activities related to the other job groups within your curriculum field.

The integrating or connecting strategies are arranged

according to general academic subject areas.

Because students may puzzle about the relationship of skills taught in regular courses and skills needed for successful job performance, a circle of careers related to a given subject area is included at the beginning of each subject area. Students should consult *The Work Book, I Can Be Anything, The Men's Career Book*, and the *Occupational Outlook Handbook* to learn more about the skills required for most careers.

General Strategies for Promoting Career Education in the School

Some of you will really get into career education and want to do more than integrating your subject area. You may want to initiate programs in your school, working in joint activities with other educators, parents, and community agencies. For those of you who want some traditional general career education activities that have worked very well in other schools, there follows a list of activities to get you started in a basic career education program for your school.

Career Day

The most successful career days are usually those which include students and teachers in both planning and implementing. For example, in planning career days around each academic department, the teacher can first develop a list of job titles that use that school subject. Students check off the jobs that appeal to them and the kinds of questions they want answered. Using this list as a basis for the community resource people to be contacted, the teacher starts a community file for potential speakers.

Careful coordination among teachers, counselors, and resource people will assure success. The speakers must know the kind of information to present as well as when and where to come. Before the speakers arrive, students should discuss potential questions to ask. Following the career day, the teacher and class should thank the speaker by letter, and ask the students for an informal evaluation.

You may want to conduct a traditional kind of career fair (where the various subject area speakers come together in a large hall), but the departmental career day described concentrates on relating school subjects to occupations—a useful object for a career education program. Here is a suggested procedure for career day.

1. Survey students in terms of careers in which they are interested in securing firsthand information.
2. Schedule the program for early in the fall of the year.
3. Open the program to all levels from 9 to 12. The major response will most likely come from juniors and seniors.
4. Assign students to meet with the representatives of the careers mentioned by the students in the survey.
5. Suggested program and timetable:
   a. Depending on the size of the school, you could schedule two or three sectional meetings.
   b. Timetable
      1) 6:00–6:30 p.m. Orientation for representative and students
      2) 6:30–7:30 p.m. Coffee and snack
      3) 7:35–8:00 p.m. Section I
      4) 8:05–9:30 p.m. Section II
      5) 9:35–10:00 p.m. Section III
6. Stress advance publicity—use the public address system, bulletin boards, school and local press, verbal encouragement from the other teachers.
7. A practice that helps to establish rapport between visiting representatives and local staff is a pre–career night buffet supper.
   a. Often parent organizations are eager to assist.
   b. Try to match local staff members with visiting representatives in terms of the occupation interests of the staff.
   c. Staff members should serve as hosts to the representatives during the evening.
8. Send a letter of information to all representatives.
   a. State the purpose of the program.
   b. Enclose a copy of the program.
   c. Secure their confirmation of attendance.
9. During the orientation period at the time of the program, stress the following:
   a. Students and representatives are to be at the assigned station at the designated time.
   b. Representatives will be furnished with a list of the students who are to be in each session.
   c. All representatives should be introduced and the name of the company with whom the representative is

affiliated mentioned. (Some will probably be private business representatives.)

Career Day Check List

1. Plan publicity: public address system and local press
2. Send reminders to staff members
3. Print name tags
4. Move parents and students from section to section by the public address system
5. Provide coatracks for guests' coats
6. Display a chart listing hosts and representatives and program schedule
7. Order programs; the art class, paper staff, or some other group could take care of this
8. Place a sign over the doors of the rooms to be used
9. Send thank-you notes to the representatives
10. Schedule picture-taking by the school paper and area press if possible

Developing a Local Audio-Visual Career Resources Library

Before career resource speakers come to the school (or when students leave for field trips), you can ask interested students to audiotape or videotape the proceedings. By filing these in the career resource center, teachers may use them with individual students, group sessions, or for classroom activities. Organizing a library of this sort is less expensive than buying commercial materials and has the double advantage of providing locally significant information while encouraging student participation.

Exchange Program

If you have friends teaching in schools in different parts of the country, you might exchange occupational information so that students can see regional differences in the way work is done and in kinds of life styles. Cassettes or videotapes of work interviews can be swapped. Newspaper clippings and "help-wanted" advertisements relating to local jobs can augment the exchange package.

Local Educational and Employment Survey

Basing a study on your subject matter and the subject areas of other teachers, you can show on a chart which local colleges and universities offer courses, majors, or specialized training in these fields. Another chart might outline local employment opportunities according to the above fields. Both kinds of information are especially useful to senior high school students when they look for summer and part-time jobs, as well as for planning their future educational and career decisions.

Bulletin Boards

Bulletin boards can be used in the classroom, in the library, in a career resource center, or in any gathering place within the school. Pictures of workers (local and nationally known), their tools and clothing, job titles, as well as articles and classified advertisements from newspapers could be combined in a collage for a specific occupation or field. With help from other teachers the bulletin board can display jobs using knowledge and skills learned in particular school subjects.

Student Resource File

Students are a ready resource concerning the kinds of jobs and volunteer activities available in the community. By sharing student experiences you can offer suggestions for other students with similiar needs. Teachers may ask students about their experiences on an informal basis or survey them by question-naire.

Games as a Teaching Strategy

Students can role-play either different jobs or famous people at work. Each student chooses a card with the name of a job or person on it. The presenter gives clues orally or through pantomime so that other students can guess the job or the famous person. After each presentation, discussion can focus on aspects such as: where is the work performed, what does the worker do, or what kind of preparation is needed?

Students can play a modified version of "Password" in pairs or in a group. One person gives a clue (about the tools, skills, duties) concerning a particular job and others must guess it. A point system may stimulate interest.

Students may play a modified version of "Twenty Ques-tions," the answer being the name of a well-known person. Questions might concern the place of residence, the job duties, the preparation required, and so on.

Another possibility is for the students to fill 3 × 5 cards with information from any career learning resource about a specific job title. Other students must guess the job title or occupational family.

Categorizing as a Teaching Strategy

Using categories from career clusters (see page 52) the students can interview workers in the community and then discuss the various ways that these and other jobs are useful. Students can further divide the job titles into categories of required personal characteristics such as the ability to: 1) be competitive, 2) help people, 3) work with things, 4) motivate others, 5) show physical stamina, 6) assume a high degree of responsibility, 7) direct the activities of others, 8) work under close supervision, 9) work as part of a team, 10) work independently.

Students should research jobs or career families and categorize their perceptions into the advantages and disadvantages of these kinds of work.

Suggest categories or settings where the jobs are performed (e.g., college, advertising agency, studio, department store, hospital). Students then list or discuss the workers employed in these settings, their responsibilities, levels or kinds of training, and interrelationships.

Develop hypothetical people endowed with special interests, skills, needs, educational plans. Students can then discuss the categories of jobs or work that these hypothetical people might find satisfying.

Develop situations concerning hypothetical students planning their careers. Give background information and bring students to a decision point (volunteering for the armed services, going to college, getting a job). Students then write an ending to the story.

CLASSROOM STRATEGIES

Integrating Strategies for English-related Careers

1. Have the class look at the range of English-related careers on the career circles on page 81. They can select two to four English careers that sound interesting to them. Assign Activity 2, "Acquiring Research Skills for Career Exploration," in About Work — Phase II, page 43. For research resources see: *I Can Be Anything: Careers and Colleges for Young Women, Men at Work: College and Career Choices for a New Age, The Work Book: A Guide to Skilled Jobs,* and *The Occupational Outlook Handbook.*

2. Assign the classroom activities in Column A, which connect naturally to career information in Column B.

Column A	Column B
Fiction or nonfiction reading assignments whose central or secondary theme concerns work	Acquiring information about jobs Occupational clusters Aspects of careers Attitudes about jobs
Discussions of lives of particular literary writers, journalists	Preparation for career skills Acquiring and advancing in occupations Income sources Outlook for writing jobs Use of writing skills in other jobs

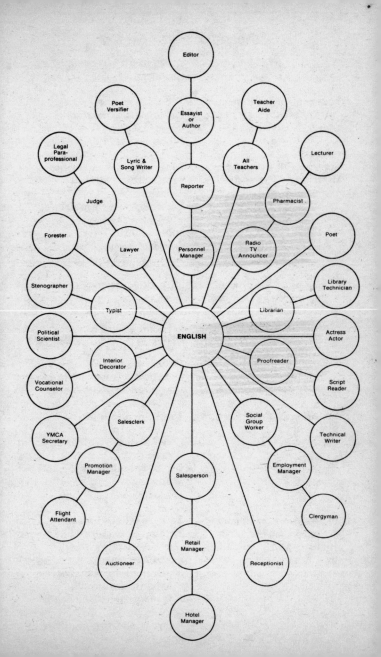

	Leisure activities enhancing career
Discussions of the impact of printed material on public policy, behavior, tastes	Job tasks of editors Qualifications of editors Career ladders Moral and ethical conflicts
Discussions of the differences in writing styles according to purpose, audience	Kinds of writers and editors Free-lance vs. salaried income Varied sources for obtaining work Job outlook Attitudes about jobs Adaptability needed in jobs
Discussions of the process by which a writer's idea gets turned from a manuscript into the printed newspaper, magazine, or book page	Necessity of teamwork in many jobs Vocabulary specific to job group Emerging occupations through technological and other changes Qualifications for and tasks of business occupations
Units on mechanics of writing, grammar	Tasks, qualifications of editors, proofreaders Preparation for writing careers Use of writing skills in other jobs Job outlook
Composition assignments requiring editing of other students' work, rewriting own work	Tasks, qualifications of different kinds of writers, editors Attitudes about jobs: satisfying different needs for different people Acquiring and advancing in jobs Reliance on work of others

Discussions about the factors and people influencing students' decisions about what they read

Tasks and qualifications of critics/reviewers, librarians, and teachers
Role of various business occupations
Impact of public taste on job outlook
Moral and ethical conflicts
Stereotyped notions about occupations

3. From Robert Caldwell's article "Career Education in the English Classroom," assign the following related readings:

Unit One: "Who Am I?"

The Unknown Citizen, W.H. Auden
Shadow Ran Fast, Bill Sands
Self-Reliance, Ralph Waldo Emerson
A Summer's Reading, Bernard Malamud
The Catcher in the Rye, J. D. Salinger
Paul's Case, Willa Cather
Miniver Cheevy, Edward Arlington Robinson
Demian, Hermann Hesse
Jonathan Livingston Seagull, Richard Bach
Ah, Wilderness! Eugene O'Neill

Unit Two: "What Do I Want Out of Life?"

Life without Principle, Henry David Thoreau
Two Tramps in Mud Time, Robert Frost
Money, Carl Sandburg
Land, Sinclair Lewis
Kindly Unhitch That Star, Buddy, Ogden Nash
Working, Studs Terkel
Waiting for Lefty, Clifford Odets
Death of a Salesman, Arthur Miller
Rabbit, Run, John Updike

Unit Three: "What Is There for Me to Choose From?"

The Secret Life of Walter Mitty, James Thurber
Dolor, Theodore Roethke
The Poverty of the Bowery, Michael Harrington
Cassandra, Edward Arlington Robinson
Quality, John Galsworthy
The Man with the Hoe, Edwin Markham
The Adding Machine, Elmer Rice
Manchild in the Promised Land, Claude Brown
Think, William Rodgers
A Student in Economics, George Milburn
Beyond the Horizon, Eugene O'Neill
Babbitt, Sinclair Lewis
Jazz Country, Nat Hentoff

Unit Four: "What Happens When I Get the Job?"

Learning the River, Mark Twain
Judge Selah Lively, Edgar Lee Masters
Under the Lion's Paw, Hamlin Garland
The Jungle, Upton Sinclair
Jack London, Sailor on Horseback, Irving Stone
All My Sons, Arthur Miller
Where I Come From People Are Polite, William Saroyan
Report from Engine Co. 82, Dennis Smith
In Chains, William Carlos Williams
The Peter Principle and *The Peter Prescription*, Laurence J.
    Peter and Raymond Hull
Horatio Alger, Jr., Frederick Lewis Allen

4. Assign the Sunday classified advertising section of a
   metropolitan newspaper to see what kinds of jobs are
   available for writers, and then have students list these
   jobs, categorizing them as literary, journalistic, specialized (dividing jobs among the subcategories of specialized writers). Also have them look for jobs not advertised
   specially as writing jobs, but which mention the need for
   writing skills. Make a list of these kinds of jobs.

5. Have the students make a chart of a career ladder for a newspaper publication and one for a book publishing house. Discuss in class the requirements for entry-level jobs. Talk about which entry-level jobs have opportunities for advancing and which are considered "dead end."

6. Assign a student to write to appropriate professional associations to obtain a code of ethics (available for advertising, journalism, public relations). Have students find examples of advertising, public relations, and journalistic writing that do not seem to fit the code of ethics. Then have them write to the person or company that originated the apparently noncomplying work to get an explanation.

7. Ask students to look in your school and community library (and also check with parents and their friends) for magazines and journals related to various writing fields to see if these magazines are helpful in terms of a career choice (for example, *Editor & Publisher, Writer's Digest*). Have them make a list of ways in which any particular magazine is helpful.

8. Ask students to consult *Writer's Market, Writer's Handbook,* and *Literary Market Place* to see the variety and numbers of publication possibilities that exist.

9. Have students bring to class a copy of as many different magazines and journals as can be obtained to show different markets for literary writing. An English or creative writing professor at a nearby college can assist, especially by providing copies of the less well-known journals that publish literary writing.

10. Interview or invite to class a free-lance writer whom students can ask about publication possibilities and other aspects of free-lance writing as a way of earning a living. Have the students plan specific questions beforehand. They should take careful notes at the interview. Then they can choose one of the following ways in which to present either the whole interview or information from part of it:

    Poem
    Short story
    Brief biography
    One-act play for theater
    Short play for radio
    Lyrics for a song

News article as prepared by an objective news
   reporter
News release prepared by a public relations writer
Newspaper feature
Humorous news column
Critical review about the writer's work
Entry in *Who's Who* or *Contemporary Authors*
Advertisement about the writer's work

11. Assign a brief written article about the same event for
    three different kinds of audiences, such as the *New York
    Times Magazine* section, *Reader's Digest*, and *Playboy*.
12. Ask the class to compare two write-ups of the same event
    to see if both examples are objective; have them write a
    short description of an event at school from two different
    points of view, each prejudiced in a different direction or
    in some way inaccurate.
13. Have the class examine local newspapers carefully to see
    how many different kinds of writers are employed. They
    should try to decide whether the journalists are salaried
    or free-lance by observing newspapers over several days.
    Then call or invite for a class visit the editor (or an editor)
    to describe staffing for news writing. Ask about which
    person has actual control over editorial content, the
    attitude of the paper.
14. Ask the students to write one class issue of a newspaper
    that includes different kinds of journalistic writing:

    —Front-page news reporting (major school news)
    —Feature article (for example, student who has
       done something special, special school workers
       such as custodians or reading specialists)
    —Review of new movie in neighborhood or recent
       school performance or art exhibit
    —Social events article (school dance)
    —Sports article
    —Articles about neighborhood or community
       news and state and national news
    —Comic strip
    —Crossword puzzle
    —Mock advertisements
    —Realistic classified ads (example: "For free
       kittens, call _____").

15. Have the class make a chart showing the career ladders in an advertising agency.

16. Ask the class to look at mastheads of newspapers and magazines to make a list of different kinds of editing jobs. They can make a hypothetical organization chart of editorial staff. Have them write to a major newspaper or magazine publisher requesting an organizational chart and compare this with your own hypothetical chart. The request may be answered more quickly if you write on school stationery.

17. Assign the Book Review section of the *New York Times* and advertisements from book clubs to see what kinds of books are being advertised and reviewed. Make some general comments about why an editor might have chosen to publish a particular book, particularly in relation to the intended audience. Examine best-seller lists for both hardcover and paperback books. Notice different categories of books, and make general comments about why each might be on the best-seller list, and why the editor might have chosen to publish it.

18. In your community library, have the students read *Publishers Weekly, Folio, The Writer, Writer's Digest*, and other trade journals that appeal to editors. Have them look at classified ads, placement and other sections to see what kinds of jobs are available, what qualifications are required for applicants, and what is being published. They can report to class on job market trends.

19. Invite an editor from a weekly newspaper and a department editor (sports or local news, for example) from a metropolitan daily newspaper to class to discuss their jobs. Having both at the same time will sharpen the students' understanding of the similarities and differences in these two kinds of editing jobs. The guests should come prepared with questions to discuss, such as tasks performed, competencies and characteristics required, education and experience required, conflicts encountered, bases upon which editorial decisions are made.

20. Make a list of writing problems (e.g., wordiness, clichés, grammatical errors, lack of clarity, misspellings). Ask the class to write a page, using a particular form (e.g., news article, short story, technical paper), aimed at a particular audience. At the top of the paper, they should

specify the form and audience. Then they should write the page of material as badly as possible. For instance, ask them to use a lot of jargon and big words in a news article aimed at a lay audience—or a lot of simple, imprecise words in a technical article. Each student should edit another's work, pointing out the problems.

21. Ask the class to draw a chart showing the general steps in publication from the author's manuscript to the reader's purchase of a book.

22. Assign a mock letter from a literary agent that tries to convince an editor to publish a book that might not sell very well.

23. Ask the students to write a mock memo from a book publishing editor to the head of the production department, who has just announced that production costs must be kept down. The editor is trying to convince the production manager why a new art book deserves high-quality printing, paper, and color photographs. The mock memo should take into account the sales market for the art book.

24. Invite to your class an employee from a publishing house, such as a yearbook representative, to discuss cost factors that affect publication and thus work for writers, editors, and other business workers. If no book publishing company is located nearby, someone from a university press that publishes books could be an excellent resource. A commercial printer also will have some notions of costs related to book publishing.

25. Invite to your class a local newspaper editor to describe the business aspects of newspaper publishing. After-wards ask the class to draw a chart showing the different jobs involved. They can write a very brief job description (with tasks, qualifications) for each business job on a newspaper.

26. Invite a newspaper business manager or controller to discuss with the class the costs of publishing a newspaper and the sources of income. Ask about the outlook for newspaper publication in the future, especially regarding job possibilities.

27. Invite a community or school library staff person to class to talk about how the staff decides which new books to buy, how the library learns about new books. Discuss with your class the ways librarians' choices of books to

purchase can affect writers and the reading public.

28. Invite a bookstore owner or manager to class to talk about the job itself and about general business aspects of bookstores. Again, have a class discussion about how bookstores can affect the writer and the reading public.

29. Have the students make a list of the last five books they have read and write a brief sentence about why they read them. Then they should list five books they would like someone to give them. Again, why did they pick those books? Were they recommended to them? Did the advertising catch them, or the cover illustration?

30. Invite a teacher, a librarian, and somebody who reviews books to class to talk about their jobs as educators in the writing field. After the guests have left, discuss whether members of the class would like doing the different jobs. Your guests should be given a list of questions prior to the visit. Suggestions are:

    a. How do the tasks performed in each job help people decide what to read?
    b. How do people get these jobs?
    c. What are the social and moral considerations in the job?
    d. What do such people like or dislike about their jobs as educators in the writing field?
    e. How available are the jobs?

31. Assign the *Columbia Journalism Review* and other journalism journals to see what topics or problems are being discussed in relationship to newspapers and magazines. Have the students choose one topic, such as reporters' embellishing of news, and find examples from several articles in newspapers and magazines that illustrate that topic. Have them write a review for a general reader indicating which of the articles they would recommend for reading. Have them use quotations from the articles to show why they would recommend some newspapers and not others.

32. Assign a short book review column to be written for the school or community newspaper. Ask students to read a number of reviews in nationally prominent newspapers and magazines to prepare themselves for writing the reviews. The column can include brief reviews of several

books, or a longer review of one book. Ask them to try to
find out whether their column has encouraged readers to
read those books they recommended.

Integrating Strategies for
Social Science-related Careers

1. Have the class look at the range of social science-related
   careers on the career circles on page 91. They can select
   two to four social science careers that sound interesting
   to them. Assign Activity 2, "Acquiring Research Skills
   for Career Exploration," in About Work — Phase II,
   page 43. For research resources see: *I Can be Anything:
   Careers and Colleges for Young Women, The Men's
   Career Book, The Work Book: A Guide to Skilled Jobs,*
   and *The Occupational Outlook Handbook.*
2. Ask the students to choose a career as a social scientist
   that is most closely related to their interests. Discuss how
   educational preparation in each of the other social
   sciences and in history would be an asset to their career.
   How would foreign language ability be a help in this
   career?
3. Have the class list entry-level jobs where social science
   graduates (four-year college) might find work—for
   example, personnel and management trainees, research
   assistants, insurance adjusters, paralegal assistants.
4. Discuss food consumption (and nutrition) in different
   areas of the country. Ask the students to consider and
   briefly outline the ways in which each of the following
   would approach a study of food consumption. For
   example, a political scientist would want to know about
   laws and the food programs of government agencies.
   Political Scientist   Historian   Anthropologist
   Economist   Geographer   Sociologist

History

1. Have the student watch a TV show, movie, or play that is
   set in the past. Discuss historical elements of dress,
   setting, speech, and events. Consider how a historian
   might have helped with the production.

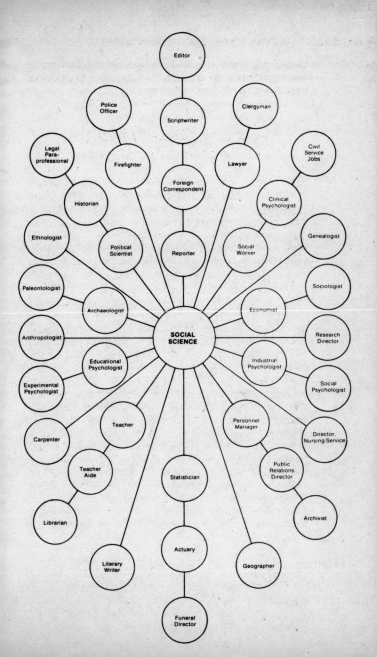

2. Take the class to a local historical society. Talk to the employees about their responsibilities, their work schedules, and their own interest in local history (students can prepare questions ahead of time).

3. Ask the students to assume that, due to budget cutbacks, they have lost their job as a college history professor. Have them write a letter applying for work to two other places (other than schools) where their education, skills, and experience would be put to use.

4. Give the students an idea of the basic settings where historians work, and various methods of reporting or presenting complete research or work; select a method of reporting appropriate to each setting.

   Ask them to choose the method of presentation and the setting most compatible with their particular combination of skills, interests, and personality. They can give reasons for their choice in a brief oral or written report.

   Example:

Setting	Method
School	Lecture
Government	Write a journal article
Museum	Compile a catalog or bibliography
	Prepare an exhibit

5. Discuss the use of technology in various jobs open to historians and archivists. They might research the use of computers (for statistical work, for programming bibliographies, for simulating alternatives open to various figures of history at certain critical times). Preservation techniques and methods of dating and authenticating material should also be considered.

   Research on computer programs will have to be carried out in the library or by consulting the math or computer programming teacher or someone in the computer business. Information on carbon 14 and phosphorescence dating methods might be obtained from the science teacher, or through library research.

6. Suggest jobs and leisure time activities for high school graduates where some knowledge of historical research methods would be an asset—for example, secretary in a

publishing company, teacher aide, tour escort. Hobbies might include reading historical novels, visiting historical museums and societies.

7. If your class thinks a historian's or archivist's work is in no way related to their life or interests, ask them to consider the following sources of historical information about themselves:

    a. Documents that could give factual information about their life—birth certificates, medical records, school records, tax forms, real-estate records.

       Discuss places where these documents are stored, such as municipal or county clerk's offices, and school departments.

    b. Sources of personal information about themselves—photos, diaries, interviews, possessions, correspondence.

       Discuss how a historian might integrate the information gained from a) and b) above to give a full picture (or a limited view) of their life.

8. Ask your class to write a brief chronological outline of their lives, giving a capsule account of events considered most important. Then:

    a. Compare and contrast types of events considered important by different students.

    b. Consider if these events would have been as important several years ago. Will they seem important five years from now?

    c. Discuss how personal viewpoint may affect a historian's work.

9. Have your students select a decade for study within the lifetime of their parents. Report the results of this study to the class.

Discuss the idea that history is also about living people. Choose topics for special study in another decade—for example, food prices, jobs available, popular music, clothing styles.

The students might talk with someone who lived through the chosen decade, read a fictional account of the period, read a textbook account of the period, or consult newspapers and magazines of the time.

Their report to the class should include a discussion of the different evidence a historian uses and evaluates and how knowledge of many specific topics is combined to give a total picture of an era. They should point out which type of information gathering they found most helpful.

10. Ask the students to construct a family tree through as many generations as possible. Careful notes should be kept to indicate various ways in which information was gained, through search of town records, through family conversations, and photographs.

11. Visit a local cemetery and project a capsule social history of a certain period from the information gained. Consider the following:

   —Names (families still in town, ethnic origin)
   —Dates
   —Inscriptions
   —Decorative style of headstones
   —Type of stone used
   —Wreaths placed by veterans

12. Have the class write to the State Department of Education or Historical Commission and request a list of places of historical interest in your area. Visit a local historical site or historical society. Talk to the employees about their responsibilities, their work schedules, and their own interest in local history.

   Students should have several basic questions prepared before the visit. (Notify the director of the historical site before your visit.)

13. Have two students role-play a discussion between an archivist with a collection of rare documents and a historian who wants access to the documents. Consider the responsibilities of each.

   For example—Archivist: "I cannot allow you to handle these documents; they are originals and not replaceable." Historian: "These documents contain information that is not available elsewhere; these facts are vital to my research. Seeing them in the original also allows me to study the paper they are printed on."

14. Since jobs in history are scarce, it is helpful to see the various opportunities for other than full-time work. Invite to class:

   a. Someone who has retired from the field of history
   b. Someone new to the field

c. Someone who works part-time in the field

Before visitors come to class, you should discuss general questions you wish to ask all visitors and particular questions you may wish to ask one visitor only.
For example, you might ask the retired person:

—What do you do to stay active in the field?
—Have history occupations changed over a period of years?

A person new to the field might be asked:

—How did you choose a history occupation?
—Was there much competition for your job?
—How did you find your job?
—How can you get ahead?
—Are there activities outside your paid work that help you in your work?

A person working part-time might be asked:

—Did you choose to work part-time? Why?
—If part-time work is not your choice, what are the problems of finding full-time work?
—Where else, outside history occupations, might you look for work?

You also might be interested in talking to someone who works in another field, but who maintains an active interest in history. You might ask this person:

—Are there opportunities for volunteers?
—What local historical sites or issues are of particular interest?

Anthropology

1. Ask each student to list their school courses and give a brief reason why each course would (or wouldn't) have some applicability to training as an anthropologist.
They might study and briefly outline some contribu-

tions of anthropological studies to our knowledge of evolution, language, and history. (Suggest some relevant books on these topics.)

2. Have the students observe the physical arrangement of your classroom or that of other rooms in your school. Discuss (or briefly list) what the arrangement suggests about the educational process. For instance, seldom used objects are in out-of-the-way places. Seats in rows may indicate one kind of activity, seats in a circle another kind of activity. What is different about the arrangement of the art, drama, or music rooms?

3. Ask the students to imagine that they are archaeologists. As part of their most recent study they must observe and make notes about a common household object. Notes should include the following information about the object:

> Dimensions
> Shape, color
> Decoration, if any
> Function
> Location where found
> Relation to other objects found

As part of their notes they may wish to include a drawing of the object. Other students might attempt to identify the object from information given, without looking at the drawing.

4. Have the class imagine that each is an anthropologist awakened from a sleep of one hundred years. From observation of a household object, draw conclusions about our society.

Objects might include paper cups, an electric toothbrush, clothing, a television set, a faucet. Conclusions could include statements about technological advances, increase in the speed of living, increased wealth, and social changes. Ask them to be careful to base their conclusions on identifiable evidence.

5. Briefly outline the duties of an anthropologist working as a teacher, museum worker, or public (government) archaeologist. Consider the advantages and disadvantages of each position. Ask the class to select the setting that is compatible with their own interests, abilities, and personality and give reasons for their choice.

6. Have the class imagine that a new job requires them to move from a very cold to a very warm climate. Briefly (in an oral or written report) have them consider resulting changes in food, clothing, recreation, personal budget, personal relations. They should assess their own ability to adapt to these changes.

7. In the field of linguistic anthropology ask your students to consider either special expressions or words that have different meanings to a small child, a teenager, an adult between thirty and fifty, and an adult over sixty-five.

   Have them construct a mini-dictionary either giving meanings for special expressions such as "really" or comparing the differing meanings of a single word such as "senior" for someone aged sixteen and someone aged sixty-six.

8. Assign the creation of a new anthropology job in business. They must convince their future employer of their expertise, the value of their services, the applicability of anthropology to current problems, and their desirable personal characteristics.

9. Debate orally or discuss in a written report the pros and cons of the following topics, which illustrate some areas of conflict in anthropological professions:
   a. Invasion of privacy versus professional responsibility in anthropological study
   b. Removing objects from the country of origin to place them in museums in another country
   c. Pressure to produce for those paying for field study versus need to do slow and careful research
   d. Value of the research and findings described in the reports of several archaeological digs or anthropological field studies

Economics

1. Have the class clip and bring in articles about economics from the local and national newspapers and magazines. Note how many times in a day economic issues are mentioned in radio or television news broadcasts. Then:
   a. List terms often used by the media in discussing economic issues. Do the students know what they really mean? A list of such terms might include "wholesale price index," "cost of living increase,"

"unemployment," and "prime interest rate."

    b. Consider and discuss the influences of the national or local economy on their lives and budget and that of their family. Do national problems have any relationship to local food and oil prices, mortgage and rental rates, or local employment?

2. Let the students imagine they are an economist employed by a manufacturer. Have them write to two other places seeking employment and mention two ways in which their skills could be put to use.

3. Choose a product that all students are familiar with (such as chewing gum, soda, and ball-point pens).

    a. Have the class construct and carry out a market research survey of students concerning product use. They should decide what questions they wish to ask about a product such as brand name, price, and reason for use. They should also decide what information they wish to have about survey respondents (school grade, spending money, susceptibility to advertising) and about other external influences on them (school rules, and parents' choices).

    b. Tabulate responses to the survey or arrange them in a way that answers informational needs.

        The number of responses, percentage of responses, and percentage of respondents not answering particular questions should be considered. Answers to each question may be tabulated.

    c. In an oral or written report have the students cite leading brands and any conclusions they have reached about reasons for their popularity. They should support their conclusions with figures from the survey. Figures may be presented as part of the narrative (75 percent of girls preferred . . .) or in table or graph form.

4. Ask the students to investigate and outline the structure of your town or city government and then decide upon the amount of funds available for a yearly budget.

    a. Small groups of students could represent each department of local government. Each group should request a portion of the total budget to meet departmental needs.

    b. Assuming that departmental demands exceed supply, departments should attempt to establish priorities and bring budgets within workable limits. Conflicts between departments (e.g., between police funding and educational funding) should be resolved in the same manner in which they are resolved locally.

c. Again, assuming that demands exceed the funds available, the class as a whole could discuss new sources of revenue in future years.

5. Have your students ask various people in the community on what basis they are paid. Consider annual salary, hourly wages, piecework, free-lance workers, and self-employed people who charge fees. Communal living, barter systems, jobs offering room and board might also be considered. Briefly outline various payment bases and consider the effect of each basis for payment upon work habits and way of life.

6. Assign a group of students to call, talk with, or correspond with a large national company, a large local company, a small local business, and someone who is self-employed. Inquire about fringe benefits offered employees. Construct a chart of the benefits offered.

The class as a whole should first discuss what fringe benefits (such as health or life insurance plans, educational aids, pension plans, vacations, paid holidays, merchandise discounts, and bonus payments) they wish to inquire about. The economic impact of these benefits both for the employer and the employee should be considered.

If businesses are reluctant to give the students information, have them talk with their parents about the benefits offered on their jobs.

7. Ask the students to pick a setting in business, banking, or government compatible with their own interests and abilities, and outline two tasks that they as an economist would like to carry out in the setting chosen.

If they are interested in business they could create a marketing plan for a new product. The environmentally conscious could outline the cost of pollution control to government. Those interested might invest winnings from the state lottery. They can be as imaginative or as conventional as they wish, but the tasks outlined should be realistic.

8. Have the students imagine that they are an economist employed by a business manufacturing automobiles (or

any other product). Outline various economic factors in automobile production. For instance, consider:

> Supply of steel
> Workers and wages
> Markets for cars
> Price and profit
> Influence of oil prices, pollution laws, etc.

Choose one factor that they think most important and recommend a consequent course of action to their imagined employer. (A company interested in quick profit will produce cheaply and sell as high as the market will pay. A company interested in pollution control will necessarily produce a higher priced car or put funds into research on electric motors.) Various choices of important factors and consequent recommendations for action could be compared and contrasted.

9. Topics for oral or written discussion:
    a. The economist in U.S. domestic politics—interrelationship of politics, economics, and family budgets
    b. Use of statistics by economists to support conclusions that agree or conflict with their own personal views
    c. The economist and international relations—fluctuations in supply and demand of natural resources and their effect on international relations
    d. Is the role and influence of economists today too great or too small?

Geography

1. Ask your students to pick a local project, such as a new road, a planned recreation facility or school, a business that is moving. Have them identify the elements of the project that would concern a geographer.

    They might also contact the local governmental department or business in question and ask if a geographer or planner is employed to help with the project. If so, what are his or her responsibilities?

2. Compile a list of words denoting geographic features

peculiar to your part of the country—for example, bayou, levee, prairie, bottomland, desert. Ask the class to consider the effect of these geographic features in producing a distinctive way of life.

3. Ask your students to identify from newspapers, current events magazines, and radio and TV news coverage current international problems a geographer might help with.

Discussion could include the exchange of natural resources, such as grain and oil, border disputes like that in Berlin, starvation in Africa, the population explosion in India, and natural disasters such as earthquakes and floods.

4. Geographers work in schools, in government agencies, in businesses. In each general area have the class choose a specific setting such as a 9th grade geography class, a coffee-importing business, the Defense Mapping Service. They can make a chart outlining two or more tasks a geographer might do in each setting. Indicate the setting each would choose as a geographer.

5. Have your students imagine that they are a geographer who has worked for several years for the zoning board of a suburban community. They would like a change of scenery. Make them write two letters: one for a job that they describe and consider a promotion; one for a job that would offer advantages different from those of their current position, but not necessarily a promotion.

You might compare a number of these letters to see how different people view promotion and job advantages differently.

6. Have your students describe the geographical elements of their "ideal" place. Consult an atlas in the library or a road map to find out if such a place exists. Note how different maps give different information about an area. Discuss the tasks of cartographers in making a single map that gives many kinds of information.

Students should note how various maps indicate topographic and climatic features as well as population density and cultural features.

7. Assign to the class a study of the interrelationship of geography and work availability in a particular area of the United States.

They might construct a map of job availability within their state and relate that information to geographic features such as natural resources, transportation availability, good farmland, and recreational features. The State Department of Labor should be contacted for employment statistics.

8. If some students are interested in computers, they might study the use of computers in map making. If they are interested in science they might study how meteorological instruments are used by geographers. Science teachers could help find information. The students can report their findings to the rest of the class.

9. Topics for oral or written discussion:
   a. What can geographers do to protect or exploit natural resources?
   b. Can geographers plan future land use?
   c. Is the work of a geographer or planner more important in urban or rural areas?
   d. Does the everyday work of geographers fit the *National Geographic* image?

Political Science

1. Ask your class to briefly outline and discuss the information a political scientist would need to understand your local government.

   Discussion could include governmental structure; boundaries of precincts, counties, state representative and senatorial districts; the background of elected and appointed officials; the demographic makeup of the town; sources of town funding; relationships with state and federal agencies; the influence of local groups such as labor unions or environmental groups.

2. Assign a poll of students in your class on a political issue. Have them present the results of the poll in graphic form. Discuss ways in which political scientists use information gained from polls.

   The poll may simply ask what political party affiliation or nonaffiliation students might choose. More complex polls might relate student choice to the choice of their parents. Other poll questions might center on local political issues such as new taxes.

3. Choose an elected official who represents your area. On the basis of information from newspaper accounts, the official's office, and the official himself, get your student

to prepare a short political biography. Include formal education, early exposure to and involvement in politics, the decision to run for office, any change in political processes or views since election.

4. Have the class describe several possible tasks of political scientists employed as teachers, government policy analysts or researchers, legislative aides. They should relate their knowledge of the tasks required to their own abilities and then choose the position or setting in which they would be most successful, giving reasons for their choice.

5. Outline areas of specialization in political science, such as voter behavior and international relations, and have your class choose the area most suited to their interests and personality.

6. Ask the class to watch newspapers for reports of a bill in the state or federal legislature that particularly interests them. They should cut out and save articles about the bill and write to your representative inquiring about the bill's support. They can comment on the likelihood of the bill gaining passage from a political scientist's viewpoint.

7. Ask your students to talk to people who do not work in political science about the work of political scientists. You might talk with other students not familiar with careers in the social sciences, with parents, and with local government employees. Questions might include:
   a. Can you name two tasks performed by political scientists?
   b. Where do political scientists work?
   c. Is their work important? Does it in any way affect your life?
   d. What kind of a personality do you think a political scientist has?

   In an oral or written report ask your students to compare and contrast the opinions of others with their own opinions and knowledge of a political scientist's occupation.

8. Topics for oral or written discussion:
   a. Advantages and disadvantages of a career in political science
   b. Various tasks a political scientist could do as part-time work
   c. Political science as a hobby

    d. Is the influence of political scientists on government policy too great or too small?

    e. Do political scientists have an obligation to make their research results available to the public?

Sociology

1. Have the students list their school courses and give a brief reason why each course would (or wouldn't) have some applicability to training as a sociologist.

2. To give them some of the nature of a sociologist's work, have the students identify different roles they live in life and the groups they belong to as they carry out the various roles:

    Daughter/son—family
    Student—school
    Citizen—community
    Worker—employees

They should briefly characterize their relationship to the group and their expected behavior in each role they have cited. Then ask them to discuss whether a change in one of their roles would have any effect on the other roles; whether there are times when they are uncomfortable with the behavior expected of them; and whether there are times when their roles conflict with each other.

3. Have the students identify and gather information on various groups in your community, and then examine the effect of these groups upon each other and on the community as a whole. Possible choices for study would be: professional groups; church groups; environmental, cultural, or recreational groups; political groups, labor unions, and so on.

    Have the students decide what they wish to know about such groups. Suggest information to gather:

    Purpose of group
    Group organization (president, secretary)
    Profile of members (number of members, age, jobs, income, and education)
    Function in community
    Influence in community

    Students might compile tables or construct graphs

illustrating answers to a specific question and compare answers between groups. The class as a whole might draw conclusions about group relationships, such as the effect that the number of members can have on the group's impact on the community as a whole.

They might also want to consider how many people belong to more than one group or inquire about the attitude of one group toward another (e.g., what do the Democrats think of Republicans). They might also discuss changes in individual groups over a period of years.

4. State some stereotypes about jobs (all doctors are rich, all artists are emotional, all clergy are self-righteous). Have the students examine facts about the careers in question by interviewing practitioners so that they can support or refute the stereotype. Discuss possible causes for the formation of stereotypes and cite instances where their use is helpful or harmful.

5. Ask your class to consider various ways in which society has changed since their parents were their age. Discuss the possible reasons for change and the conflicts caused by change.

They might focus on one aspect of social change such as laws, technology, social customs, or politics. They might talk with their parents and other adults or draw information from the publications, music, and art of twenty-five years ago and today.

6. Briefly outline some "norms" used by students in your school. You might consider generally accepted classroom behavior, behavior in the halls, behavior at a school social function, speech and gestures used with teachers, speech and gestures used when talking with other students, modes of dress. Do these "norms" differ for males and females?

Discuss what happens to the student who departs from norms or who does not act as teachers or students expect.

7. Have your class watch for news of national opinion polls in the newspapers or on TV and bring examples of information on polls to class. Discuss:

   a. Variety of topics covered by polls
   b. Method of collecting opinions for the polls (if any is given)

    c. Way in which poll results are presented—as tables, graphs, narrative, etc.

    d. Advantages and disadvantages of polls in indicating national opinion.

8. In an oral or written report have all the students pick the job setting for sociologists most compatible with their own interests and personality. Have them give reasons for their choice. Outine two questions about society that a sociologist (in the setting chosen) would try to answer.

Integrating Strategies for Agriculture-related Careers

1. Have the class look at the range of agriculture-related careers on the career circles on page 107. They can select two to four agricultural careers that sound interesting to them. Assign Activity 2, "Acquiring Research Skills for Career Exploration," in About Work — Phase II, page 43. For research resources see: *I Can Be Anything: Careers and Colleges for Young Women, The Men's Career Book, The Work Book: A Guide to Skilled Jobs,* and *The Occupational Outlook Handbook.*

2. Have the students describe ten careers in the field of agribusiness.

3. Ask some students to interview various people employed in farm machinery sales.

4. Ask interested students to describe at least ten careers directly involved in the forestry industry.

5. Have students report on how agricultural clubs and activities can lead to knowing more about agricultural careers.

6. Ask the class to bring articles from newspapers and magazines to class dealing with current conservation problems, and discuss careers related to these social problems.

7. Have all the students choose the career in agriculture that is most closely related to their agricultural interests. Discuss how educational preparation in their other high school subjects would be an asset to this career.

8. List wildlife management jobs and have the class discuss the educational preparation for each one.

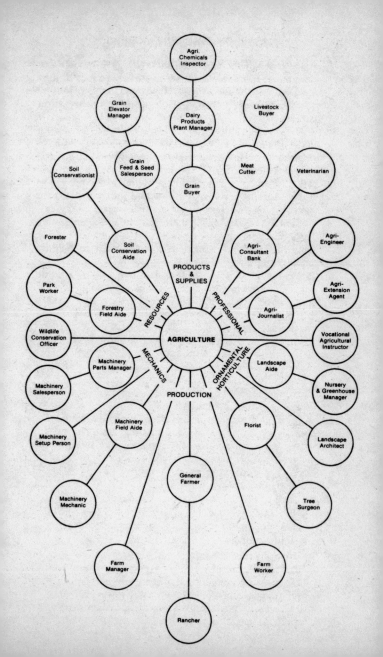

9. Assign the Sunday classified advertising section of a city newspaper to enable students to see what kinds of jobs are available for agriculture. Have them list these jobs by categories such as farming, agribusiness, conservation careers.

10. Ask the class to make a chart of a career ladder for an extension agent. Talk about which entry-level jobs have opportunities for advancement and which are considered dead end jobs.

11. Ask the students to look in the school and community library for the trade magazines and journals listed on pages 52–54 for agriculture-related careers. They can make a list of ways in which the particular magazine may be helpful.

12. Make a chart showing the career ladder in wildlife management.

13. Have the class look at the classified ads in a trade magazine to see what kinds of jobs are available, what qualifications are required for applicants, and what is being published. They can report to the class on job market trends.

14. Have your students make a list of five books that include agricultural careers in them.

15. Take a class trip to a fish and game department, a slaughterhouse, a veterinarian's practice.

16. Have some students take pictures of workers on different jobs as the tour progresses.

17. Agricultural education revolves basically round six major job families: (1) production agribusiness, (2) agricultural mechanics, (3) supplies and services, (4) agricultural products, (5) horticulture, and (6) forestry. Ask your students to place the following careers in the proper job family:

Landscape architect	Machinery salesperson
Petroleum engineer	Livestock buyer
Wildlife manager	Florist
Fish and game manager	Farmer
Agricultural engineer	Ranger
Golf course manager	Tree surgeon
Soil conservationist	Dairy farmer
Water systems service	Veterinarian
representative	Butcher

Equipment service representative	Miner
Feed store manager	Farm manager
Extension agent	Agronomist
	Forest ranger

18. Invite an animal nutritionist to speak to the class after a visit to a cattle feedlot and class observation of different rations for cattle.

19. Invite a turf management specialist and an extension horticulturist to speak on the investments required to start a plant nursery.

20. Invite a chemical salesworker to speak to students on "Careers in the Field of Fertilizers." Include local fertilizer distributors and liquid nitrogen plant workers.

21. Have students report on the sales and services of fertilizers, pesticides, machinery, chemicals, seeds, and feed.

22. Have them research and report on the operation and function of the four basic agricultural lending agencies— Production Credit Association, Federal Land Bank, Intermediate Credit Bank, Farmer's Home Administration.

Integrating Strategies for Visual Arts and Crafts-related Careers

1. Have the class look at the range of visual arts and crafts-related careers on the career circles on page 110. They can select two to four visual arts and crafts that sound interesting to them. Assign Activity 2, "Acquiring Research Skills for Career Exploration," in About Work —Phase II, page 43. For research resources see: *I Can Be Anything: Careers and Colleges for Young Women, The Men's Career Book, The Work Book: A Guide to Skilled Jobs,* and *The Occupational Outlook Handbook.*

2. Exploration in visual arts and crafts careers can be connected to the content of the following courses in the ways suggested:

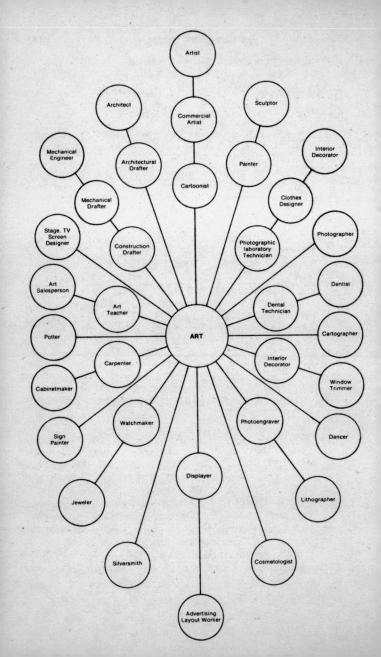

General Arts Course	**Connecting Strategy**
Found-object sculpture	Introduce the role of product designer by talking about the found objects and what they were designed to be. Who designed them? How?
Sketching	Introduce illustration as a career by having students sketch ideas to illustrate some specific material.
Pottery making	Introduce production crafts by organizing the class into a production studio to turn out multiple editions of their clay designs.
Drafting	Introduce the educational process of an aspiring architect by having students design and make models of simple buildings.
Watercolor painting	Introduce fine arts by having students attempt to show their paintings in the community.
Montage	Introduce graphic design by having students prepare their montages as book cover designs.
Museum visit	Introduce criticism by having students review an exhibition.

Class exhibit	Introduce arts business and management by having students publicize and mount their own exhibit.
Printmaking	Introduce commercial printing and sign designing by having students print signs or broadsides for a school event.
Photography	Introduce journalistic photography by having students propose specifications for photo essays of the school's history.

Visual Communications

3. Ask your students to look around for examples of visual communications. Find as many kinds (from bookplates to billboards) as you can. They can make a scrapbook or poster of these examples and separate them by type, such as: illustrations from graphic designs, from cartoons, from calligraphy. Discuss the different kinds of professionals who worked on those designs.

4. Arrange your class, or groups within the class, into an imaginary design studio. Have the students "consult" for a museum that needs a newsletter published. You could explore with the class the relationship of graphic design to other fields by playing such roles as:
   a. Museum director, who will direct the overall focus of the newsletter
   b. Business manager, who will set the budget
   c. Technical copywriter, who will write the articles to be illustrated

   Students in the "design studio" could choose very specific roles, such as photographer, type designer. Which people have steady jobs? Which would work freelance? Who has more authority? Who earns more? Lead a discussion on some of the differences between the design professions.

5. Find a "want" ad in the paper that calls for someone with

art skills. Cross out the part of the ad that describes the specific job being advertised, so that the ad reads something like this, "someone with experience in drafting and paste-ups to work in large office as assistant director." Have the class guess what the job could be, what kind of work that person would do and what kind of office it is. The ad could be for an architectural drafter, an industrial designer, an assistant in a cartoon studio, or for any one of dozens of jobs. Discuss the fact that some skills, such as drafting, can be used in all sorts of jobs.

6. At the end of a semester, or a unit, discuss the different kinds of "jobs" students may have held during that time. If, for example, they drew a picture one day and lettered a poster the next, they held two jobs—one as an illustrator, one as a calligrapher. Do artists ever change jobs like that? Discuss the idea of a career being made up of many jobs.

7. At the beginning of a class unit, students should choose a professional role to play. If, for example, they are making posters, the role could be as the art director of a publishing firm. What does this entail? Is the work full-time? Who are the art director's subordinates and boss? How does one apply for the job? Have the students report to the class on the job and its advantages and disadvantages.

8. Lead a discussion based on questions such as:
   a. What does an illustrator (graphic designer, display artist) do?

      —Is he or she licensed to practice?
      —Does she or he work alone?
      —What exactly does he or she do at work?
      —What training does she or he need?
      —How does he or she earn a living?

   b. Would you want to be a graphic artist?

      —Could you do it well?
      —Are you competitive enough?
      —Are you "visual" in your thinking?
      —Would you like to work under pressure?

   c. If the class were to put out a magazine, what would you have to do?

—Would you need a photographer? What would she or he do?

—Who would direct all the work?

—Would you all work alone, or in teams?

—Do you need anyone except artists to work with you?

d. What effect does graphic design have on society?

—Do visual advertisements affect our buying habits?

—Do we read only the leaflets that look "good"?

—Do we judge a book by its cover?

—Do we look at colorful ads before black and white ads?

—Are we attracted by elaborate packages, regardless of what's inside?

—Is there such a thing as a "modern" look?

—Do graphic styles change according to changes in trends in other art fields?

Product Design

9. If possible, invite a product designer to the class, or take the class on a field trip to a designer's office. Prepare questions to ask. Discuss with the class what they expect a product designer's job to be like *before* the visit, and discuss their preconceptions again *after* the visit. Does the product designer work alone? Does he or she really "invent" things? Does she or he make actual products, or just plan them? How does the product designer's job differ from the student's image of that job?

10. Design the form of a package with the class. This can be an interesting project if the product to be packaged is unwieldy, such as a canoe, a whole set of dishes, or a live chicken. Perhaps you could design one package to hold all three items. This could be related to graphic design if you also decorate the package and make it look marketable. Discuss the role of some product designers such as specialists who do only one kind of work, such as packaging. What other specialties could a designer develop? Would a specialist work for a manufacturer or

could he or she work free-lance? What training would she or he need? What skills?

11. Make up an imaginary budget for mass-producing a class project. For example, if the class is making pottery, make up a budget for a commercial production of 1,000 sets of these pots. The students should ask themselves some of these questions:

—How much time did it take to design the pot?
—Would you pay the designer by the hour? How much?
—Whom would you pay more—the designer or yourself? Why?
—Whom else would you have to hire?
—Which people would have to work at the factory? Which would work at home?

12. Lead a discussion or make the students prepare a report on cultural differences in product design: find examples of products that are considered very good in one culture and very bad in another. For instance:

a. Would we consider a Japanese hard pillow a well-designed product? Would they think our soft pillows are good?
b. Would a European who pays $2 for a gallon of gas think a Cadillac is "good"?
c. Would we think an oriental dining table on eighteen-inch legs was "good"?
d. Would we still think a Model T was a "good" car?
e. Would we think a washboard was as modern and efficient as our great-grandparents did?

What effect will our culture have on the future for product designers? Are people's careers entirely in their own hands, or do they have to "take their chances" as society changes?

13. Lead a discussion based on questions such as:

a. What would you like to design and how would you do it?
   —What would you have to know to be able to do it?

—Where could you get such a job?

—What qualifications would you need?

b. What "things" in this room were designed?

—What did a designer have to know about each thing to design it?

—What else would the designer have to work with?

Environmental Design

14. If possible, invite an environmental designer to the class, or visit a designer's office. Prepare questions to ask. Have the class discuss what they expect a designer's job to be like *before* the visit and discuss their preconceptions again *after* the visit.

—Is that person's job as "glamorous" as they expected?

—Does he or she do the kind of everyday work they expected?

—What kind of education did she or he have?

—What other ways could his or her skills be used?

15. Make the students find an environment they *don't like* and redesign it. They should keep a record of the steps they took in redesigning the space.

—Was the actual work all artistic?

—Were some of their decisions made for practical reasons?

—Which aspects of the work did they like? Why?

—Are the skills they used similar to those they have used in other classes? How?

16. Ask some students to design a landscape without any buildings. The landscape can be urban (such as a playground) or natural (such as a park). It should be designed to serve some specific purpose. The students could also do this by redesigning an existing, familiar landscape.

Ask the students questions such as:

—How is landscape architecture different from other kinds of design work?

—How would a landscape architect prepare for her or his career?
—With whom would a landscape architect work?
—For whom would a landscape architect work?

17. Have each student work with a friend in class to set up an architectural contract. One of them should play the role of a client and present the specifications of a house he or she wants to build. The specifications could be difficult, such as a swimming pool in the bathroom, or a dance floor in the kitchen. Then they should draw up plans for the client's "ideal" house. Then you should discuss with them:

—Is this how a real architect works?
—Is this how a real client would act?

18. Lead a discussion based on questions such as:
   a. How would you organize yourselves in a "full-service" design studio?

   —Would you need an architect?
   —Would you need a landscape architect?
   —Would you need an engineer? What kind?
   —Would you need an interior designer?
   —Would you need an urban planner?
   —What would each of you be responsible for?

   b. How can environmental design affect our lives?

   —Do we feel better in well-designed spaces?
   —Is "better" always more expensive?
   —Would we live differently in a different kind of space?
   —How do different places affect our behavior?
   —Are some places easier to keep clean? to light? to keep warm? Why?

Fine Arts

19. Visit a museum or an art gallery. Have your students describe their experience to the class.

—Were the works of art they saw by contemporary artists?
—Do they suppose the artists sold their work directly to the museum?
—Do they suppose the artists are wealthy?
—Do they suppose the artists work full-time on their art?

20. Ask your students to look at various big-city newspapers to see how many articles there are about visual arts.

—What are these articles about? Are they criticisms of art shows, or simply reports about these shows?
—How many articles are there? Does art get as much coverage as sports or television?
—What effect do they suppose this lack, or excess, of coverage has on individual artists?
—Does it seem easy to students now for an artist to become famous?

21. Have some students attempt to "show" a piece of their artwork. They can go through the process that an artist goes through: bring a portfolio of their work to galleries; find out where amateur shows are being held; apply for admission to professional art associations. They should report to the class about their experiences. Do students think that many artists can support themselves solely by showing and selling artwork? What else must they do?

22. Organize a show of work done by students in your class. Each of them should choose a professional role to play in this project, such as an exhibition designer, gallery director, framer, or critic.

23. Have your students check your local newspaper for art-related jobs. They should imagine that they are an artist looking for a part-time job to support themselves.

—Are there many jobs to choose from?
—Might the artist have to take a nonrelated job?
—Do they think that many artists have exactly the same jobs, or the same combination of jobs?
—Are artists' careers likely to be very individualized?

24. Have some students visit a fine arts-related business such as:

A framing shop
An art school
A government-sponsored art foundation
An art supply store

With help from you, they can arrange to talk with some
of the employees about their work at these places.

25. Lead a class discussion based on some important aspects
    of a typical artist's career. Try to include some facts such
    as these:

    a. The art public (those who buy original art and
       frequent galleries) is very small.
    b. New York is the center of the art world.
    c. Galleries take up to 60 percent commission.
    d. Many shows charge entrance or hanging fees.
    e. Galleries take on only a few new artists each year.
    f. Artists rarely get royalties on their work when it is
       resold at a profit. The profit is split by the dealer
       and the collector, and not the artist.
    g. There are other outlets for exhibiting besides
       commercial galleries, such as cooperative galler-
       ies, community museums, and bank lobbies.
    h. Artists work on speculation, producing work that
       may not be sold.
    i. Artists work alone.
    j. Most artists work in series.
    k. Art is a one-of-a-kind production.
    l. Artists do *not* work to please the public.
    m. Artists cannot separate their work from the rest
       of their lives.
    n. Artists improve with maturity. It is not a field for
       child prodigies.
    o. Fine arts are not so well represented in media
       coverage as movies and sports.
    p. Individual grants to artists are rare and usually
       small.
    q. Exhibitions do not necessarily result in sales.
    r. Artists usually support themselves by taking other
       jobs.
    s. Very few artists ever support themselves by sales
       of their work.

You might introduce this discussion by raising some
questions such as:

—How does an artist become known?
—If you were a young artist, how would you support yourself?
—Does society appreciate artists?
—What are the advantages of being an artist?
—What are the disadvantages of being an artist?

Perhaps you could raise such questions a few days before you lead a discussion, to give the class a chance to think about the answers.

Crafts

26. Have your class visit a craftsperson's studio. Ask the craftsperson several questions about his or her career, such as:

    —How much time do you spend on a single piece of work?
    —Do you design all your own work?
    —Do you produce more than one copy of each piece?
    —Do you work in more than one medium?
    —Do you work in series of similar pieces?
    —Do you have any other jobs, or do you support yourself with your craft?
    —Do you cooperate with any other craftspeople in either buying materials or selling your work?
    —What training is needed to become a craftsperson like yourself?

27. Have your students organize a show of class crafts work. Everyone should choose a professional role to play such as a gallery director, critic, or exhibition designer.

28. Get some students to attempt to sell a piece of their crafts work. Have them find out if there are any professional crafts organizations or cooperatives in your area. If there are, they should ask members for advice in showing crafts work in your area.
    Discuss with the students questions such as:

    —Are there many ways to sell crafts work?
    —How would you price your work?
    —Could you actually make a profit after deducting the cost of your materials and the time you put in?

—Do you know of any famous craftspeople?
—Can craftspersons earn a living in your area?
—Do people consider crafts important?
—Do people consider crafts a "fine art"?

29. If possible, have the class visit a crafts-related business. This could be:

A crafts supply house
A crafts cooperative office
A design office at a textile mill or wallpaper mill
A crafts school

You can help the class arrange to talk with some of the people who work there.

30. Lead a discussion based on a typical craftsperson's career. The discussion could cover such points as:

   a. The public for crafts (those who buy original pieces) is small.
   b. There is no real center of the crafts world as there is in the art world.
   c. Commercial crafts galleries charge a commission.
   d. There are other outlets for showing and selling besides galleries.
   e. Crafts cooperatives are becoming very popular.
   f. Craftspersons frequently work on speculation, producing work that may never be sold.
   g. Craftspersons frequently work alone for long periods.
   h. Craftspersons do *not* work to please the public, but to satisfy themselves.
   i. Craftspersons do not separate their work from the rest of their lives.
   j. Craftspersons improve with maturity and experience.
   k. Crafts are not so well represented in media coverage as other art forms (e.g., movies, theater, etc.).
   l. People do not always want to pay for high-quality crafts goods.
   m. Individual financial grants from arts councils to craftspersons are rare and usually small.
   n. Craftspersons frequently support themselves by taking other jobs.

Arts Business and Management

31. Invite someone in the arts business and management field to speak to your class. If possible, have the class prepare interview questions beforehand. They might ask questions such as:

   —Does your job have a title? What is it?
   —Where do you work?
   —Did you know ten years ago that you'd be a _____ today?

32. Ask your students to look through the local Yellow Pages and make a directory of all the cultural institutions, arts organizations, and art-related businesses listed. Categorize different types of entries (i.e., separate art supply stores from galleries and historical museums from contemporary galleries). Discuss differences between the categories. This might also be a good time to lead a class discussion based on this activity. You might ask questions such as:

   —Is there more or less art activity in town than you expected?
   —If there are professional artists in town, are there any organizations listed that could really help them? How?
   —Are there any institutions listed that you never heard of before? Why hadn't you heard of them?
   —Have you visited any of these places? Why? Why not?
   —What kinds of people work in these places?

Integrating Strategies for Biology-related Careers

1. Have the class look at the range of biology-related careers on the career circles on page 123. They can select two to four biology careers that sound interesting to them. Assign Activity 2, "Acquiring Research Skills for Career Exploration," in About Work — Phase II, page

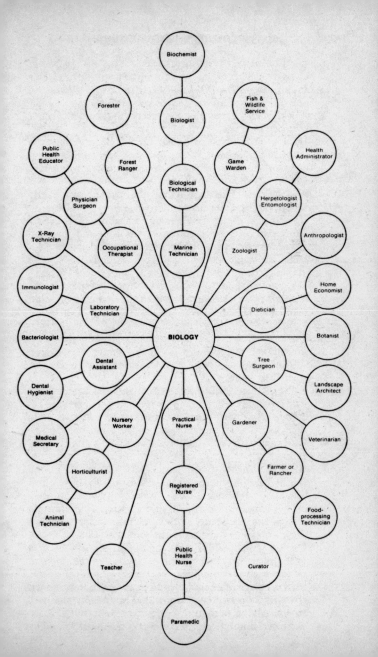

43. For research resources see: *I Can Be Anything: Careers and Colleges for Young Women, The Men's Career Book, The Work Book: A Guide to Skilled Jobs,* and *The Occupational Outlook Handbook.*

2. Ask the class to describe ten careers in the field of plant science.

3. Have some students interview various people employed in plant science such as a feed and seed salesworker, elevator manager, farmer, feedlot manager, nursery worker.

4. Ask the class to describe at least five occupations directly involved with soil science.

5. Have a group interview people on the job, such as Soil Conservation Service personnel, fertilizer and chemical salesworkers, and fertilizer truck operators.

6. Have students report how science club or science activities could lead to learning about science careers.

7. Have each student bring articles from newspapers and magazines to class dealing with current conservation problems. Discuss careers related to these social problems.

8. Discuss: How is a pharmacy, a grocery store, a photographic studio, a hearing-aid dealer, a television station, the parks department, a print shop, a hospital related to biology?

9. Hobbies often lead to a career. Most local hobby shops will give your the names of some scuba divers who will come and present their observations as well as explain their gear. After studying marine life and observing an aquarium with your students, invite a scuba diver to your class.

10. Have the class research newspapers for new legislation that is being proposed on health problems for workers (tie in special health hazards for your own locality—e.g., brown lung, nuclear radiation, industrial air pollution).

11. Assign some students to research population increases for all major countries for the past ten years.

12. Discuss land pollution. What is the importance of a garbage worker? Ask the class to report on attempts to use garbage to make fuel.

13. Plan a replica of an underwater city. Assign class reports on what an underwater city would be like. Include jobs that would be necessary.

14. Tour the health career section of a technical school.

15. Ask the students to choose the career in biology that is most closely related to their science interests. Discuss how educational preparation in each of the other sciences and mathematics would be an asset to their career.

16. Have each student list entry-level jobs where biologists with a master's degree might find work.

17. Assign the Sunday classified advertising section of a city newspaper so that students can see what kinds of jobs are available for biologists. Have them list these jobs by categories such as business, research, academic. Also ask them to look for jobs not advertised specially as biology jobs, but which mention the need for science skills. They can make another list of jobs of this kind.

18. Have some students make a chart of a career ladder for a botanist in a frozen foods company. Discuss in class the requirements for entry-level jobs. Talk about which entry-level jobs have opportunities for advancement and which are considered dead end jobs.

19. Ask interested students to write to the professional associations to obtain a code of ethics. Discuss the implications for ethics in the sciences in class.

20. Have your class look in your school and community library for the trade magazines and journals listed on pages 52–54 for biology-related careers. They can make a list of ways in which a particular magazine is helpful.

21. Make the students write a science article for three different kinds of audiences catered for by the science magazines they find.

22. Ask interested students to make a chart showing the career ladder in college teaching.

23. Assign the classified ads in a trade magazine so that students can see what kinds of jobs are available, what qualifications are required for applicants, and what is being published. Have students report to the class on job market trends.

24. Have some students make a list of five books that include a biologist.

25. Have students who collect insects, seeds, butterflies, and other biology-related collections report to the class.

Integrating Strategies for Chemistry-related Careers

1. Have the class look at the range of chemistry-related careers on the career circles on page 127. They can select two to four chemistry careers that sound interesting to them. Assign Activity 2, "Acquiring Research Skills for Career Exploration," in About Work — Phase II, page 43. For research resources see: *I Can Be Anything: Careers and Colleges for Young Women, The Men's Career Book, The Work Book: A Guide to Skilled Jobs,* and *The Occupational Outlook Handbook.*

2. Have the class describe five careers in the field of energy.

3. Ask some students to interview various people employed in food science.

4. Assign a description of at least ten occupations directly involved with the petroleum industry.

5. Have students report on how science club or science activities could lead to learning about science careers.

6. Ask students to bring articles from newspapers and magazines to class dealing with current recycling problems. Discuss careers related to these social problems.

7. Discuss: How is a pharmacy, a grocery store, a photographic studio, a hearing-aid dealer, a television station, the auto parts department, a print shop, a hospital, an oil refinery related to chemistry?

8. Ask students to choose the career in chemistry that is most closely related to their science interest. Discuss how educational preparation in each of the other sciences would be an asset to their career. How would mathematics help?

9. List and discuss entry-level jobs where chemists with a master's degree might find work.

10. Assign the Sunday classified advertising section of a city newspaper so that students can see what kinds of jobs are available for chemists, and then have them list these jobs by categories such as business, research, academic. They should also look for jobs not advertised specifically as chemistry jobs, but which mention the need for science skills. They can make another list of jobs of this kind.

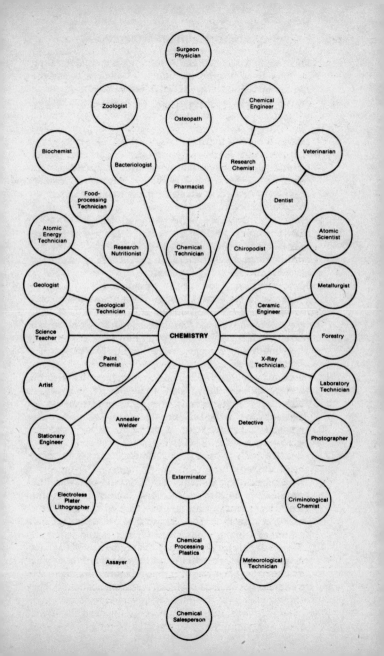

11. Have some students make a chart of a career ladder for a chemist in a plastics company. Discuss in class the requirements for entry-level jobs. Talk about which entry-level jobs have opportunities for advancement and which are considered dead end jobs.

12. Ask interested students to write to the professional associations to obtain a code of ethics.

13. Ask the students to look in the school and community libraries for the trade magazines and journals listed on pages 52–54 for chemistry-related careers. They can make a list of ways in which the particular magazine may be helpful.

14. Have your students write a science article for three different kinds of audiences catered for by the science magazines they find.

15. Ask interested students to make a chart showing the career ladder in college teaching.

16. Have the class look at the classified ads in a trade magazine to see what kinds of jobs are available, what qualifications are required for applicants, and what is being published. They can report to the class on job market trends.

17. Have interested students make a list of five books that include a chemist.

18. Take class trips to a medical research center and oil refinery and emphasize the activities of the workers.

19. Ask interested students to take pictures of workers on different jobs as the tour progresses.

20. Organize a science club with emphasis on students developing science hobbies.

21. Create a bulletin board on chemistry careers for your classroom.

22. Have chemistry students do a study of labels on containers in the kitchen, medicine cabinet, and cleaning closet. Get them to learn about a limited number of the substances on the labels. Those that are identified will fall into a number of chemical categories and will open many channels for discussion. The students will find out about the interrelatedness of chemistry with everyday life and the workers who manufacture and sell the products.

Integrating Strategies for Commercial and Distributive Education-related Careers

1. Have the students look at the range of commercial and distributive education-related careers on the career circles on page 130. They can select two to four commercial and distributive education careers that sound interesting to them. Assign Activity 2, "Acquiring Research Skills for Career Exploration," in About Work —Phase II, page 43. For research resources see: *I Can Be Anything: Careers and Colleges for Young Women, The Men's Career Book, The Work Book: A Guide to Skilled Jobs,* and *The Occupational Outlook Handbook.*

2. Ask the class to look up and describe the following commercial education-related careers:

Accountant	Keypunch operator
Secretary	Salesperson
Office manager	Bookkeeper
Personnel director	File clerk
Advertising worker	Purchasing agent
Computer operator	Computer programmer
Public relations worker	Stenographer
Bank manager	Bank teller

3. Have some students interview various people employed in a department store.

4. Ask the class to describe at least ten occupations directly involved with the fashion industry.

5. Have students report on how distributive education clubs and activities can lead to knowing about merchandising careers.

6. Have students bring articles from newspapers and magazines dealing with current inflation problems and discuss careers related to these problems.

7. Ask the class to choose the career in commercial or distributive education that is most closely related to their interests. Discuss how educational preparation in each

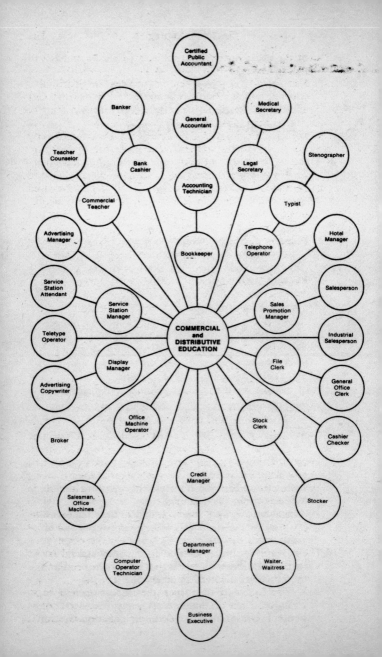

of the other high school subjects would be an asset to their career.

8. List entry-level jobs where commercial or distributive education high school graduates might find work. List another group of jobs where students with two years of college might find work.

9. Assign the Sunday classified advertising section of a city newspaper so that students can see what kinds of jobs are available for commercial students, and then have them list these jobs by the amount of education they need to get them. Also ask them to look for jobs not advertised specifically as commercial or distributive education jobs, but which mention the need for these skills. They can make another list of jobs of this kind.

10. Ask the class to look up and describe the following distributive education-related jobs:

Sales representative	Sales supervisor
Statistician	Sales engineer
Advertising representative	Systems analyst
Bank teller	Hotel-motel manager
Transportation manager	Media buyer
Marketing researcher	Credit manager
Packaging designer	Finance manager
Production and control manager	Realtor
	Insurance agent
Customer service agent	Cashier

11. Near the end of a class period, ask students to select by consensus a common item from the classroom environment. It may be a desk, a pencil, a picture on the wall, or any other specific item. Tell students that the following day they will trace that item from its origins to its place in the classroom by naming every occupation that is necessary to bring it there. Ask them to think about the problem overnight, to talk to others about it, and to jot down some specific ideas so that they can construct a complete occupational flow chart. They should try to determine the raw materials that go into the product and the processes involved in producing it.

The following day, open the discussion and begin listing all of the occupations involved. They need not be in order, but some kind of chronological organization is helpful. Insist that students be specific in naming occupations. For example, if the item selected is a pencil, they should not be satisfied with the generic term "sales representative" but should include the lumber salesperson who sold the wood to the manufacturer, the paint salesperson, the eraser salesperson, the graphite salesperson, and so on. It will not be possible to develop a complete list, but it should be extensive. When the list has grown to respectable proportions, ask students to identify all of the occupations on the list that are directly connected with marketing and distribution. Circle or star these occupations. This may stimulate suggestions for additional occupations from the class. Be sure that advertising, transportation, warehousing, and selling are included wherever appropriate.

12. Divide the class into "creative teams" and assign each team one of the student activities. (These should be general activities such as sports events or dances, as opposed to group activities such as club meetings.) Each team will develop an advertising campaign for the activity assigned to it. Have the team members designate various responsibilities to specific individuals. For example, each team will need an account executive, a copywriter, an art director, a media buyer, a production manager, and so on. The team can create posters, handouts, radio commercials, and other types of advertisements.

    If possible, the campaign should actually take place and should be tied to the event. In any case, some sort of post-event analysis should take place, with the various teams comparing their campaigns and discussing the duties of specific occupations within the team. This activity can be expanded to include market research and other related tasks if the teacher so desires. Remember, the important part of the activity is not the quality of the product or products but the experience students gain in learning about the various occupations employed in advertising, in working under the creative team concept, and in understanding the division of responsibilities in a group effort.

13. Have each student describe a sales situation in writing on one side of a sheet of paper. The description should give details of the item being sold, the location of the sales effort, and the individuals who are involved. The

description of the individuals should be as complete as possible, including ages, sex, mood or type of character, buying habits, and so on.

For example, a student might set a scene in which a young woman recently employed as a shoe salesperson in a department store is selling shoes to a middle-aged man who has spent most of the day shopping and is somewhat tired and irritable. Wherever possible, the description should be based on a real situation that has been experienced or observed by the students themselves or by their acquaintances. (Encourage students to think beyond the strict retail selling situation to include industrial sales, door-to-door sales, and other direct sales situations.)

Attach a number to each of the student papers and display them in a convenient location. Using some form of random selection, form a series of two-member teams in the class. At periodic intervals during the semester, have the teams draw a number from a hat. This number will indicate the sales situation that the team is to act out before the class. Give the team a day or two to think about the situation, but discourage team members from working together to perfect a performance; the object is to fully accept the roles of sales representative and customer, based on the descriptions provided.

Give each team five or ten minutes to perform, and then ask for class discussion about how the sales representative might have done a more effective job. This is particularly useful if students are learning sales techniques and can relate the performance they have witnessed to the sales techniques they have learned. This activity is primarily a career preparation activity, but it is also useful as a consumer education tool.

14. Discuss the importance of a salesperson in our economy. Include the notion that everybody sells. Use the students for examples in everyday living: getting a job, getting a date. In different careers, how do the following occupations sell: medicine, education, and religion?

15. A student can make a chart showing the career ladder for a credit manager.

16. Have another student make a career ladder for a purchasing agent in a floor-covering manufacturing company.

17. Ask an interested student to write to the professional

associations to obtain a code of ethics. Discuss the implications for ethics in class.

18. Have the class look in your school and community libraries for the trade magazines and journals listed on pages 52–54 for commercial and distributive education-related careers. They can make a list of ways in which the particular magazine may be helpful.

19. Organize a commercial education club with emphasis on developing money-making hobbies.

20. Create a bulletin board on commercial and distributive education careers for your classroom.

21. Ask your students to imagine that they are either:

> —A free-lance court reporter
> —A legal secretary
> —A paralegal

They want a promotion. Have them outline what they consider to be promotion possibilities, and also consider educational requirements. They should plot the steps toward their promotional goal.

Integrating Strategies for Foreign Language-related Careers

1. Have the students look at the range of foreign language-related careers on the career circles on page 135. They can select two to four foreign language careers that sound interesting to them. Assign Activity 2, "Acquiring Research Skills for Career Exploration," in About Work —Phase II, page 43. For research resources see: *I Can Be Anything: Careers and Colleges for Young Women, The Men's Career Book, The Work Book: A Guide to Skilled Jobs,* and *The Occupational Outlook Handbook.*

2. Ask students to choose the career from the list that is most closely related to their interests. Discuss how educational preparation in foreign languages would be an asset to their career.

3. Have the students role-play as interpreters in class, in such roles as a social worker, an airline worker, a hotel clerk.

4. Ask the class to translate any two of the following: a poem, a recipe, directions for operating an appliance, an

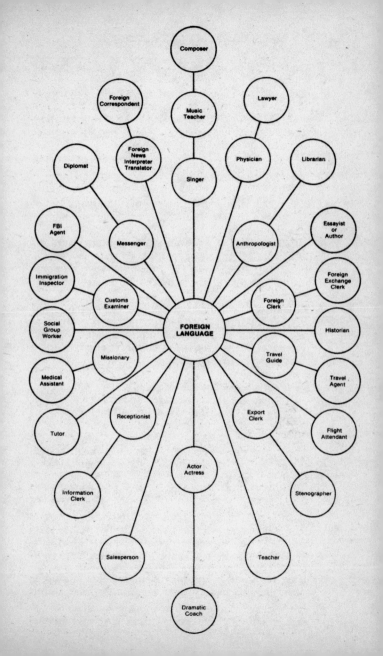

advertisement, a scientific experiment. Compare and contrast the abilities and specific knowledge needed by the translator in each case.

5. Have students role-play an escort interpreter in two of the following situations:

   —A tour of a factory
   —A party for tour members
   —Scheduling accommodations
   —City sight-seeing tour

   Comment on the special problems of each situation—the voice control needed, vocabulary, background knowledge, and personality.

6. Ask students to prepare an oral or written report on "Why I would be a better interpreter than translator" (or vice versa). They should relate their own abilities, skills, and personality to those needed by interpreters and translators.

7. Since there are very few interpreters and translators who receive a full-time salary, it is helpful to understand free-lance work. Invite to class, or correspond with, someone who works free-lance as a translator or interpreter. Some sample questions might be:

   —What does "free-lance" mean?
   —What are the advantages and disadvantages of working free-lance? How do you find work?
   —Do you get reimbursed for travel expenses?

   If interpreters or translators are not available locally, professional associations might suggest someone willing to correspond with the class.

8. Ask two students to role-play a conversation between an importer and an exporter. They should maintain the courtesies exchanged when two strangers meet. As importer and exporter they might converse in a common language or use the services of an interpreter. Discussion might include prices and shipping process. Later, you should discuss with the class whether they think business is conducted more efficiently in a common language or through an interpreter.

9. Ask a student to pretend that he or she is a politician and deliver a speech in a foreign language. Have another

student act as interpreter for the class (the class should also be able to understand the language of the politician).

This activity will be more challenging if the interpreter deliberately imposes his or her own opinions on the speech of the politician. The class should discuss the possibilities for distortion of feeling, emphasis, and fact by the interpreter and the consequences of this distortion. Students might also comment on the need for language skills in international relations today.

10. Identify a job for a person who is fluent in a foreign language and a job for a person who has some language skill in addition to other skills in the following settings: education, business, government, communications, the arts. Briefly outline the use of language skills in each job.

11. Ask an interested student to correspond with the personnel department of a large multinational corporation or an agency of the federal or state government. The student should inquire about current jobs that call for language skills and ask which languages are used most at this time and which will be used most in the next ten years. Then compare this information with what the students know about languages currently in demand. Discuss the reasons for changing demands—for example, relations with different countries, and differing patterns of world trade.

Examples of large corporations to contact might be Coca-Cola, General Motors, Exxon, Eastman Kodak. The social services division of state government might be contacted or the Foreign Service branch of the U.S. Department of State might give some interesting answers.

12. Invite to class a person who uses English as a second language. Ask him about the language-related problems of his life in this country (e.g., words that sound the same but have different meanings, slang and idioms).

A person who uses English as a second language might also be interviewed at home or over the phone. At that time, in private conversation, it might be interesting to explore whether those who do not speak English well are aware of any discrimination, either when job-hunting or in social relations. You might also discuss with the class what difficulties one might encounter when living in another country.

13. Ask the class to compile a list of words from other

languages that have become part of the American vocabulary. Words might include musical, medical, or legal terms, as well as words used in everyday conversation (e.g., "cafe," "rendezvous," "pronto," "gesundheit," "hippopotamus").

14. Compile a file of resources in the local area for a chosen foreign language. Such a file might include information on literary works in the library, foreign language publications, recordings, radio and TV programs, restaurants, cultural associations, and people who are naturalized citizens or visitors to this country.

15. Organize a foreign language club with emphasis on developing communication hobbies.

16. Arrange a trip to the nearest airport to observe personnel at work, to collect brochures, and to seek information concerning foreign passengers and foreign trade. Have the class explore the foreign language needs of the following airline personnel: flight attendants, flight announcers, ground hosts, reservation clerks, customs officers.

17. Divide the class into two groups to explore the foreign automobile industry. For example, explore and locate the French, German, and Italian auto industries. List the makes and their characteristics. Visit dealers who specialize in foreign cars. Explore the monetary exchange.

18. Ask an interested student to explore the American Overseas Auto Operation and report findings to the class.

19. Have students research famous French restaurants—both in major cities and locally. Inquire for a native French chef. Try to get an interview, take the group to the restaurant and observe all the jobs in the restaurant business, including ownership and promotion.

20. Take to class Spanish, French, German, or Italian magazines and have students point out the differences and similarities in the foreign and American advertisements. Discuss the following: What are some of the products that may be advertised in an American magazine, and not in one of these foreign magazines and vice versa, and why; what are some good factors in producing good advertisements; what are some skills that will be helpful in the career of an advertisement agent?

21. List and discuss jobs in which the knowledge of Spanish, French, Russian, German, Japanese is useful. Have students note down their ideas on the following topics: Hotels—There are more tourists in the U.S. than ever before, and only 2 percent of hotel employees are bilingual; International businesses—There are different types of businesses that need bilingual personnel, e.g., petroleum companies, jewelry companies, and purchasing agencies; Government jobs—One in every six persons in the U.S. works for the government. It is almost a necessity for a policeman and other government workers to know Spanish in New York, Florida, Texas, California, and many other states. Also, it is an advantage to know Spanish for the FBI, CIA, and other agencies for international development; Journalism—A bilingual person is indispensable for the success of some publications. Journalists also edit educational textbooks and tapes in Spanish; Professionals—The knowledge of Spanish is practical for nurses, doctors, lawyers, and other professionals who may encounter in their field some Spanish-speaking people who do not speak English.

The list of careers is longer and as many as necessary can be described.

Integrating Strategies for Shop and Industrial Arts-related Careers

1. Have students look at the range of general shop and industrial arts-related careers on the career circles on page 140. They can select two to four shop and industrial art careers that sound interesting to them. Assign Activity 2, "Acquiring Research Skills for Career Exploration," in About Work—Phase II, page 43. For research resources see: *I Can Be Anything: Careers and Colleges for Young Women, The Men's Career Book, The Work Book: A Guide to Skilled Jobs,* and *The Occupational Outlook Handbook.*

2. In woodworking, introduce furniture design by organizing groups into design teams, with industrial students responsible for designing, pattern making, and model building.

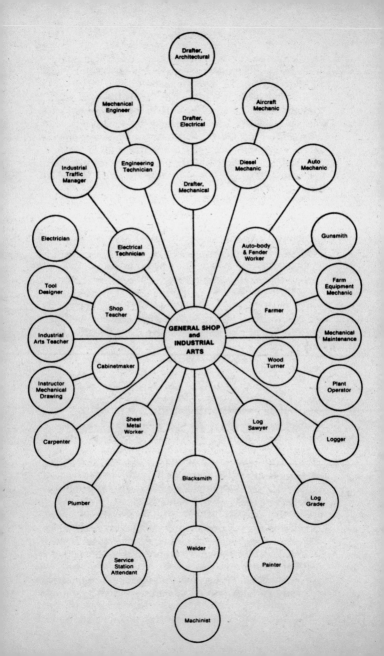

3. In mechanical drawing, introduce visual communications by having students prepare camera-ready layouts of materials for the school paper.

4. In drafting, introduce interior design by having students prepare elevations of a bi-level room plan for a renovation of the school auditorium.

5. In welding, introduce fine arts by having students do interpretive sculpture with scrap metals.

6. In plastics, introduce product design by having students create utilitarian household objects with fiberglass lamination techniques.

7. In cabinetry, introduce museum and display work by having students design display cases and stands.

8. Have some students describe eight careers in the field of woodworking.

9. Ask interested students to interview various people employed in drafting.

10. Have the class describe at least ten occupations directly involved with the automobile manufacturing industry.

11. Have the students bring newspaper and magazine articles to class dealing with current problems of high unemployment and discuss careers related to this social problem.

12. With your class, visit a local industry shop after discussing the manufacturing process from design through manufacturing, marketing, and servicing. Students should be familiar with sand molds, metal casting, hot-working mechanical processes, and cold working.

13. Have the students report the major areas of production and services within the local community.

14. Discuss the similarities and differences between skilled mechanics and operatives.

15. Discuss the similarities and differences between custom occupations and service occupations.

16. Hand out several sets of plans (architectural, civil, mechanical) for student inspection. Discuss the need for engineering drawings as a means of communicating with mechanics, craftspersons, laborers, businesspersons, and consumers.

17. Have students report on the types of engineering drawings commonly used by industry:

1. Orthographic
2. Axonometric
   a. Isometric   b. Dimetric   c. Trimetric
3. Oblique
   a. Cavalier   b. Cabinet   c. General oblique
4. Perspective
   a. Parallel   b. Angular   c. Three point

18. Have each student produce a complete set of basic house plans of his or her own design. Explain and demonstrate beforehand the process of laying out preliminary plans for home design. Stress layout ideas that tend to group areas and features so that construction costs are kept as low as possible within the desires of the customer. Discussion should include the following topics:

   1. Preparing preliminary (scaled) sketches as a means of communication with customers and working out problems
   2. Choosing a proper scale to work with
   3. Preparing working drawings:
      a. Method of dimensioning
      b. Location of and specifications for doors and windows
      c. Wall intersections
      d. Load-bearing walls
   4. Foundation plans:
      a. Footings and foundation
      b. Detail drawings
      c. Headers, sills, and joists
   5. Roof plans:
      a. Styles of roofs
      b. Rafters, ridge beams, king rafters, wind braces, and pointers
   6. Elevation views:
      a. Establishing forms and shapes
      b. Continuity of style
      c. Points of emphasis
   7. Renderings or perspectives
      a. Location and presentation of best features while not camouflaging less attractive features
      b. Shading
      c. Landscaping

8. Electrical plans:
   a. Electrical symbols
   b. Brief discussion of national electric code
   c. Local building codes and inspection process

19. Have a student make a chart showing the career ladder in cabinetry.

20. Assign the classified ads of a city newspaper to enable students to see what kinds of jobs are available for drafters, machinists, and welders. Also ask them to look for jobs not advertised specifically as these jobs, but which mention the need for these skills. They can make another list of jobs of this kind.

21. Create a bulletin board on industrial arts careers for your shop.

Integrating Strategies for Home Economics-related Careers

1. Have the class look at the range of home economics-related careers on the career circles on page 144. They can select two to four home economics careers that sound interesting to them. Assign Activity 2, "Acquiring Research Skills for Career Exploration," in About Work —Phase II, page 43. For research resources see: *I Can Be Anything: Careers and Colleges for Young Women, The Men's Career Book, The Work Book: A Guide to Skilled Jobs,* and *The Occupational Outlook Handbook.*

2. Ask the class to describe ten careers in the field of food and nutrition.

3. Have interested students interview various people in early childhood education.

4. Have a group of students describe at least ten occupations directly involved with the textile and clothing industry and report the descriptions to the whole class.

5. Have students report on how home economics clubs or activities can lead to learning about home economics careers.

6. Ask the class to bring articles from newspapers and magazines to class dealing with current child-care problems, and discuss careers related to this social problem.

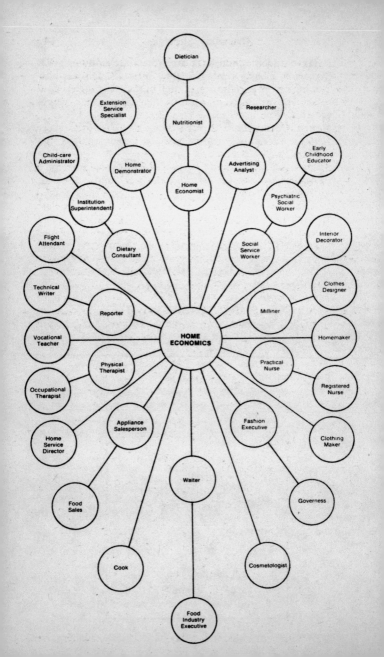

7. Have students choose the career in home economics that is most closely related to their interests. Discuss how educational preparation in each of the other high school subjects would be an asset to their career. How would science and art help?

8. List and discuss with your class entry-level jobs where home economists with a bachelor's degree might find work.

9. Have a student make a chart of a career ladder for a home economist in the fast-foods business.

10. Ask an interested student to write to the professional association to obtain a code of ethics. Have the class discuss the implications for ethics on the job.

11. Identify skills young people are acquiring in their own homes that will be valuable to them for entry jobs in various areas. Talk about transferable skills like decision making, time-management, budgeting, persuasion skills, planning and following-through skills.

12. Prepare a bulletin board giving general areas of homemaking. Use large letters placed on colored circles to spell "homemaking." Make the outline of the house in large yarn.

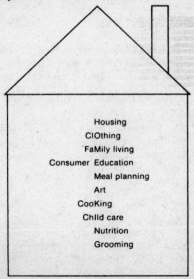

Housing
ClOthing
FaMily living
Consumer Education
Meal planning
Art
CooKing
ChIld care
Nutrition
Grooming

13. With your class, visit a day-care center or kindergarten.

Observe the children. Talk with the director after the children have gone and discuss the operation of the center, the personal qualities needed for the job, the education needed, the problems, the rewards and frustrations of the job.

14. a. Invite a fashion director to class. The fashion director for a department store can talk on modeling, preparing a fashion show, requirements for models, some exercises, makeup, the advantages and disadvantages of being a model.

 b. Take the class to a fashion show. Discuss all the jobs related to the show.

15. a. Visit and observe the operation of your school cafeteria during several class periods.

 b. Ask the lunchroom supervisor to speak to class on specific problems involved in the operation of the cafeteria and explain the equipment and procedures used.

16. Using furniture in need of repainting or repair, have students in groups of two or three study appropriate refinishing techniques and apply them to the furniture. Take students to visit a refinishing shop and discuss the job possibilities in furniture refinishing.

17. Have the students read the Sunday classified ads in a city newspaper to see what kinds of jobs are available for home economists, and then list these jobs by category of business, government, or school. Also they should look for jobs not advertised specifically as demanding a home economist, but which mention the need for home economists' skills. Have them make another list of jobs of this kind.

18. Have a student make a chart of a career ladder for a home economist in a fashion merchandising job.

19. Look in your school and community libraries for the trade magazines and journals listed on pages 52–54 for home economists and related careers. Have your students make a list of ways in which the particular magazine is helpful to them in learning about career opportunities.

20. Ask your students to look at the classified ads in the trade magazines to see what kinds of jobs are available, and what qualifications are required for applicants. Have them report to the class on the job market trends.

21. Have the students make a list of five books that include some home economics specialists.

Integrating Strategies for Mathematics-related Careers

1. Have the class look at the range of mathematics-related careers on the career circles on page 148. They can select two to four mathematics careers that sound interesting to them. Assign Activity 2, "Acquiring Research Skills for Career Exploration," in About Work — Phase II, page 43. For research resources see: *I Can Be Anything: Careers and Colleges for Young Women, The Men's Career Book, The Work Book: A Guide to Skilled Jobs,* and *The Occupational Outlook Handbook.*

2. Ask the students to list six careers that use math and investigate those occupations to establish the type of math used in them.

3. Assign each student a different type of job related to math and have the students collect information from people in their own families and community on how that particular job relates to mathematics.

4. Take a class trip to see computers in action. Students should report on a) working conditions, b) environment, c) attitudes and conduct of workers they observed and talked to, and d) how mathematics is used.

5. Have each student bring in specific data-processing instruments that are applied to everyday life. If your school uses computers for course offerings, class lists, attendance, and scheduling, use school data processing for discussion. A resource person from your school could serve as discussant.

6. Each student will illustrate the need for mathematics in the field of architecture. Using building plans and magazine ads of buildings, discuss the mathematics skills an architect needs.

7. Have each student bring a graph from the newspaper, or illustration using mathematics, and present it to the class describing how mathematics is related to the job.

8. Devise a crossword puzzle of jobs that require a

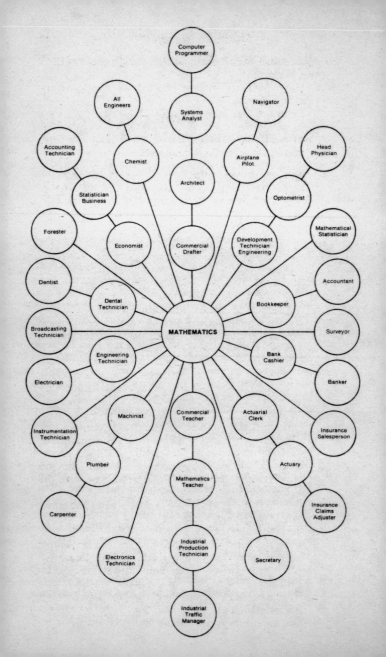

mathematics background, and have students devise their
own puzzle.

9. a. Have geometry students discuss the sizes different
rooms should be.

  b. Draw a house plan (use scale 1″ = 4′).

  c. Teach students key words: measurement, units of
measure, linear units, square units, scale measure,
actual measure, ratio, proportion.

  d. Talk about the employment possibilities in house
designing and planning.

10. a. Have a speaker from a photo shop or a print shop
describe how they use ratio and proportion.

  b. Tour the businesses in a) and also visit the newspaper
office to see ratio and proportion being put into use.

  c. List the local photo and print shops in your
community with a discussion of jobs for these
businesses.

11. a. Teach basic math students key words: utility, water
bill, water meter, cubic feet.

  b. Get rates from the local water company.

  c. Have a representative from the local water company
talk to the class about jobs in the water company.

  d. Teach the students how to read water meters.

  e. Have them draw meters for their classmates to read.

12. a. Teach basic math students key words: utility, phone
bill, phone service, limited phone service, unlimited
phone service, party line, private line, toll charges,
collect calls, listed or unlisted numbers.

  b. Have a representative from the phone company talk
with the class. Find out about the different rates, the
different time periods, the advantages and disadvantages of unlisted numbers. Find out the job
opportunities for high school graduates with the
phone company.

  c. Get a schedule of rates if it is not in the phone book.

  d. Work some phone bills.

  e. Figure the phone tax.

13. a. Teach general math students key words: simple
interest, principal, rate, percent, savings, loans.

  b. Work problems using the simple interest formula I =
PRT.

  c. Have a banker talk with the class about jobs for high
school graduates.

  d. Discuss places where simple interest is used.

14. a. Teach general math II students key words: employment, statistics, groups, percent, census bureau.
    b. Find the percentage of people employed in different occupations.
    c. Discuss the different occupations.

15. a. Teach general math students key words: measurements, standard measures, pound, ounce, pint, quart, cup, tablespoon, teaspoon.
    b. Look through cookbooks or magazines for recipes, and ask relatives and friends for their favorite recipes. Have the students double and triple the recipe amounts.
    c. Review multiplication and division of fractions in connection with this calculation.
    d. Maybe use ratio and proportion to increase the amount of each recipe ingredient.
    e. Have a quantity food cook speak to the class about changing recipes.
    f. Tour a bakery or restaurant and interview cooks and chefs.

16. a. Have students find different kinds of graphs (broken line, bar, circle) in magazines, periodicals, or newspapers.
    b. Give the students certain statistics and let them graph them on the best type of graph.
    c. Take a survey of what occupations your students wish to pursue. Use current literature to estimate the expected lifetime earnings (in your area) and the cost of education (again in your area) to achieve that career. Find what percentage of the lifetime earnings the cost of the necessary education represents. Have your students graph this data.

17. Have a programmer or a computer operator speak to the class about occupations available in your area, and also explain how different bases are used by those working with computers.

18. Have a representative from the clerical department of a nearby plant talk to the students or visit a clerical department with your class.
    a. Give students a chart with the gross pay of several workers. Let them compute the FICA deductions using their knowledge of percents, federal withholding tax, and state withholding tax using the charts available at the nearby tax office. Have the students

determine the take-home pay of these workers.

   b. Discuss other deductions: insurance, retirement, and savings.

   c. Ask students who are willing to do so to bring checks from part-time jobs. Calculate payroll deductions and see if their checks were figured correctly.

19. Have a person from the local social security office talk to the students about the benefits from social security, how to get a social security card, and the jobs available at social security offices.

20. Have students go to department stores. Have them look for sales and figure out the marked price, net price, and discount.

   a. Let one student pretend to be a salesperson and one a customer. Have the salesperson set up a sale and explain to the customer the marked price, net price, and discount.

   b. Explain the formula $p = n \times b$ and have students work problems to find net price, list price, and discount rate. Discuss sales jobs.

21. Discuss the use of the Pythagorean property in design and construction jobs.

   a. Visit a nearby house or building under construction. Have the carpenter explain how he uses the Pythagorean property in sawing roof rafters.

   b. Have a drafter talk to the class and explain his or her uses of the Pythagorean property.

22. To gain some real understanding of the practical aspects of commission, your class should visit a neighborhood business, such as a car sales lot; or you could hand out examples of car, real estate, and insurance salespeople's salaries based on commission and ask the following questions or similar ones:

   —Is your entire income dependent on commission?

   —Do you prefer to work on a commission basis? Why or why not?

   —Would you advise us to seek employment on a commission basis?

   a. Have students compute the amount of commission when the total sales and the rate based on total sales are known.

   b. Given the total sales and the amount of commission, have students compute the net proceeds.

   c. Given the total sales and the amount of commission,

have students compute the rate of commission.

23. Simulate a TV program on the topic: "Know your jobs related to math." Select class members who are to participate in the program as panel members and moderator. Brief the participants beforehand on their roles, or make them responsible for research concerning the jobs on which panel members will be quizzing them.

24. Hold a panel discussion on the topic: "Which math jobs of today were not in existence when my parents were in school."

25. Models can be the starting point for a lesson on ratio and proportion. Have the various class members bring their models to school and display them. Discuss the various jobs necessary in constructing a particular model. Example: building a ship: welder, carpenter, or painter.

26. Have each student describe five careers in the field of engineering.

27. Ask interested students to interview various people employed in statistics.

28. Ask the class to describe at least ten occupations directly involved with the computer industry.

29. Have students report on why and how math clubs can lead to learning about math careers.

30. Ask the students to bring to class articles from newspapers and magazines dealing with current automation problems and discuss careers related to these social problems.

31. Assign the Sunday classified advertising section of a city newspaper for the students to see what kinds of jobs are available for mathematicians, and then have them list these jobs by category of business, research, and government. Also ask them to look for jobs not advertised specifically as math jobs, but which mention the need for mathematical skills. They can make another list of jobs of this kind.

32. Have the class look in your school and community libraries for the trade magazines and journals listed on pages 52–54 for math-related careers. Ask them to make a list of ways in which the particular magazine may be helpful.

33. Ask interested students to describe four math-related jobs in the insurance industry.

34. Have a student make a chart showing the career ladder for a systems analyst.

Integrating Strategies for Music-related Careers

1. Have the class look at the range of music-related careers on the career circles on page 154. They can select two to four music careers that sound interesting to them. Assign Activity 2, "Acquiring Research Skills for Career Exploration," in About Work—Phase II, page 43. For research resources see: *I Can Be Anything: Careers and Colleges for Young Women, The Men's Career Book, The Work Book: A Guide to Skilled Jobs,* and *The Occupational Outlook Handbook.*

2. Exploration in music careers can be connected to content.

   —From the consumer viewpoint, discuss the workers who provide the music we hear.
   —Discuss the changing social position of musicians through history, and what that position is today.
   —When discussing different styles of music, discuss also the differences in life-styles and working conditions of the musicians.
   —Follow a musical production, keeping track of the workers involved at every step from conception to review.
   —When discussing instruments, emphasize how they are made and by whom.
   —During discussions of individual performers, groups, or orchestras, consider the management structure of each, bringing out the work responsibilities at each level.
   —When considering a specific period of music history, assess the impact of musicologists' work upon performers' interpretation.

3. Class project—community search for musical resources. Using the following sources and others that may yield information, make a catalog (or bulletin board) of the musical resources of your community. Sources of information include:

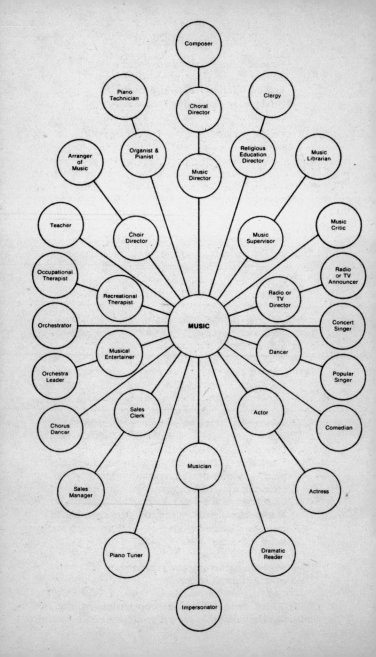

—Newspapers (classified advertisements)
—Yellow Pages of the phone directory
—List of churches that hire organists, cantors, conductors, choir directors, and singers
—List of retail music establishments from the chamber of commerce
—Students' own firsthand knowledge

Musical resources should include:

—Professional performers
—Volunteer and amateur performers
—Retail outlets
—Piano tuners
—Music teachers in schools and studios
—Recording studios
—Music section of the public library
—School music groups
—American Federation of Musicians (local)

This material can be collected over a long period, assembled into a catalog for future use, and updated as you obtain new information.

4. With your class, compile a list or directory of music-performing opportunities in your community. Divide the list into paid and unpaid opportunities. Take into account *all* places where music is performed.

—Recording studios—are the musicians hired full time?
—Churches—do they pay musicians?
—Community orchestra—are some musicians paid?
—Community chorus
—Town band
—Nightclubs—do musicians work every night or just weekends?
—School groups
—Local rock groups
—Music festivals in your region
—Special opportunities

If there seem to be few opportunities for live musicians in your area, discuss possible reasons, such as:

—Population is sparse
—Legal restrictions (against nightclubs)
—Religious considerations (some church groups
do not use music in worship)
—Lack of interest in music
—Shortage of trained performers
—Shortage of music teachers
—Lack of concert hall space

5. From the local office of the American Federation of
Musicians (AFL–CIO), or from the national headquar-
ters of AFM, 1500 Broadway, New York, New York
10022, obtain a copy of the Code of Ethics, an agreement
describing the domains of school and professional
musicians.

—Review the contents of the code
—Discuss whether or not you think the code is
necessary
—Do you think the code is fair to school
musicians? Why or why not?

6. Have some students make a line or flow chart that shows
how music gets from creator to consumer through one of
the four ways governed by the copyright law. Using the
same chart, follow the flow of money from the consumer
back to the artist.

—Who invests the money?
—Who gets the percentages?
—Who takes the greatest risks?

7. The recording business provides most of the music heard
today. Millions of dollars are spent promoting the latest
tunes. How much of the success of a tune is due to the
tune itself; how much is due to advertising and
promotion campaigns? Discuss whether or not these
statements are true, keeping in mind the current hits:

—The only difference between a hit song and a
song that is not a hit is the advertising
campaign. Success has nothing to do with the
song itself.
—If classical music were promoted in the same

way as rock music, then classical music would
be more popular.

—If the public doesn't like a song, then it won't
sell.

—The public doesn't know what kind of music is
popular or good until record companies and
disc jockeys tell them through advertising.
Advertising manipulates public taste.

8. Ask your students to listen to a television show,
preferably a rerun. They should cover the screen or turn
down the picture so that they can concentrate on the
background music. Is the music effective on its own or
does it need the picture? Try to imagine the recording
session as the music was added to the sound track. What
responsibilities would the conductor have?

9. Ask students to pretend they are an "artist and repertoire
person." Have them listen to several songs on records
and decide which one they would accept for their record
company to produce. They should justify the choice on
musical grounds, or what they feel is public taste.

10. Have each student listen carefully and consciously to
some background music in an airport, restaurant, or
other public location. Does it cover the background
noise? Is it interesting? Should it be interesting? Can it be
considered to be noise pollution? Why or why not?

11. Assign a student to write to the Library of Congress to
obtain Form Eu, which will be mailed to you at no
charge. The address is: Copyright Office, Library of
Congress, Washington, D.C. 20540. On request the
library will also send a pamphlet explaining the
copyright law. The student should report the findings to
the class.

12. Have interested students write to, call, or visit a local
radio station to get information about performing rights
payments. If they have the detective instinct, and if your
community is small enough, they might be able to find
out the total amount of money that all radio stations pay
in performance fees in your area.

13. Buy recent issues of *Variety, Cash Box, Rolling Stone,*
and *Billboard* at a newsstand. (Perhaps your public
library subscribes to these periodicals.)
Have your class look through the magazines for:

—Job openings
—New releases of records
—Lists of best-selling records
—Stories of trials and court proceedings that affect the music industry

Students can make a report to the class comparing the top ten records in *Cash Box* with the ten best-sellers in *Billboard*. Are both lists the same? Different? If different (they usually are), can the students determine *why* they are different?

Note: back issues may be obtained by writing these publishers:

Billboard, 9000 Sunset Boulevard, Los Angeles, California 90069.
Cash Box, 1780 Broadway, New York, New York 10019.
Variety, 154 West 46th Street, New York, New York 10036.

14. The American Federation of Musicians has a new program called "Young Sounds of the AF of M," an orientation and educational program for young musicians planning to enter professional music careers. Have an interested student write to the union for information and report to the class. The local office of the union will be listed in your phone directory. (See address in Activity 5.)

15. Ask one student to interview your school music director to find out:
    a. What are all the nonmusical tasks that have to be done before giving a school concert?
    b. What is the cost of producing a musical show at your school and what items are included in the cost (for instance, salary, music rental, royalties, piano tuning, set, scenery, props, costumes, printing)? They should report the findings to the class.

16. Ask a group to write a musical commercial for a coming school event. Organize talent and record the commercial. Several "takes" may be necessary to get a good version. Have it played on the public-address system with the daily announcements.

17. Have your class prepare arrangements of school songs

for publishing. Make master copies as neat as possible. Find out who controls the copyrights and find out if you have the legal right to print copies of the songs. Your school print shop may be able to make copies of the songs.

18. Have some students prepare a 15-minute radio show. Be sure that they include station breaks, commercials, news bulletins, time and temperature check, and recorded musical selections. They should find out which performing rights organization each selection belongs to and keep a log. (BMI, ASCAP, or SESAC should appear on the record label.) Timings, titles, and performing rights societies should be included in the log.

 Present the program to the class live.

19. Ask an interested student to research and report on the life, career, and death of Florence Ballard, one of the original "Supremes." They will need to consult the *Reader's Guide to Periodical Literature* and the *Washington Post* for Sunday, April 27, 1975. Tell the class whether or not Florence Ballard was treated fairly by Motown records and why.

20. A student can interview the director of a community playhouse, or theater or university theater to find out the cost of producing a musical show. What items are included in the cost? The student should report the findings to the class.

21. Arrange for the class to visit a music business work place to observe and talk with the workers. Many sites offer organized tours for groups, but other visits may be difficult to arrange.

 Possible sites include:

 —Radio and television stations
 —Recording studios
 —Music publishers
 —Record companies

You may be able to arrange a visit to the class by a concert promoter, record company executive, recording engineer, or disc jockey, who will be able to answer some questions about the music business.

Integrating Strategies for Physical Education-related Careers

1. Have the class look at the range of physical education-related careers on the career circles on page 161. They can select two to four physical education careers that sound interesting to them. Assign Activity 2, "Acquiring Research Skills for Career Exploration," in *About Work —Phase II*, page 43. For research resources see: *I Can Be Anything: Careers and Colleges for Young Women, The Men's Career Book, The Work Book: A Guide to Skilled Jobs,* and *The Occupational Outlook Handbook.*

2. Ask the class to describe ten careers in the field of recreation.

3. Have the students interview various people employed in physical education.

4. Ask interested students to describe at least ten occupations directly involved with the sports industry.

5. Have students report on how playing sports can lead to learning about health and physical education careers.

6. Assign as reading matter "Discovery through Sports," by Dr. N. M. Shepard, in *Free to Choose: Decision Making for Young Men,* and *Other Choices for Becoming a Woman* (Dell).

7. Have the students make a list of five books that include female and male athletes.

8. Have the students research the recreation agencies within their community for summer employment opportunities for high school students.

9. Have the students make posters that describe the summer recreation jobs they researched, the hours required, and possible pay scales.

10. Have the students report on the sportswear industry, including designing, manufacturing, selling, and advertising.

11. Ask an athletic trainer to visit the class and have a student interview the trainer about educational preparation and the duties of the job.

12. a. Arrange for a female and male representative of the High School Officials Association to come in and speak to all P.E. classes. They should speak on the following topics:

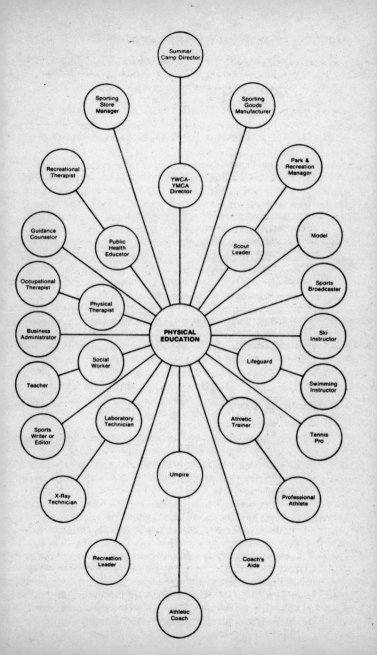

—How to become an official
—The economic values of being an official
—The responsibilites of being an official
—The problems of being an official

b. Give a short rules course on the sport that is in season (fall—football, soccer; winter—basketball and wrestling; spring—baseball).
c. After the rules course, let each student have a chance to officiate a regulation game of the sport that is in season. Class size will determine how much time each student will spend officiating.

13. Have students read the Sunday classified ads in a city newspaper to see what kinds of jobs are available in physical education and recreation.
14. Ask the students to write a letter to the Parks and Recreation Department to get information about activities offered to people of all ages in the state. Discuss the jobs available through this program.
15. a. Discuss with the students how career may affect their whole future style of living, i.e., work atmosphere, friends, and recreations.
    b. Have students research the various occupations they are interested in and list the leisure time and family life implications of each occupation.
    c. Students should report on the characteristics of occupations such as earnings, work schedule, and physical and mental exertion.
16. Discuss camping with the class:
    a. In one group have students develop a list describing the advantages and disadvantages of camping.
    b. Have another group locate all state parks on an outline map of your state and list the recreation activities of each.
    c. Have another group locate well-known lakes in the state and the recreational activities at each.
    d. Discuss the employment opportunities in all aspects of camping.
17. Have students design recreational activities for children, based on one or more of the following categories: dance, drama, music, art, nature exploration, sports or games, and animal study. The design should include such factors as cost, time required, amount of supervision required, motivational techniques, facilities and equipment, size of

group, and other considerations. This will provide valuable experience for those who are interested in recreation careers as well as for those students who will use their understanding of recreational activities for their personal and family leisure time.

Integrating Strategies for Physics-related Careers

1. Have the class look at the range of physics-related careers on the career circles on page 164. They can select two to four physics careers that sound interesting to them. Assign Activity 2, "Acquiring Research Skills for Career Exploration," in About Work — Phase II, page 43. For research resources see: *I Can Be Anything: Careers and Colleges for Young Women, The Men's Career Book, The Work Book: A Guide to Skilled Jobs,* and *The Occupational Outlook Handbook.*

2. Have your students describe ten careers in the field of electronics.

3. Ask an interested student to interview various people employed in nuclear energy.

4. Have your class describe at least ten occupations directly involved with aerospace.

5. Have students report on how science clubs or science activities could lead to learning about science careers.

6. Ask your students to bring to class articles from newspapers and magazines dealing with current radiation leak problems and discuss careers related to this social problem.

7. Ask each student to choose the career in physics that is most closely related to their science interest. Discuss how educational preparation in each of the other sciences would be an asset to their career. How would mathematics help?

8. List the entry-level jobs where physicists with a master's degree might find work.

9. Assign the Sunday classified advertising section of a city newspaper so that the student can see what kinds of jobs are available for physicists, and then have them list these jobs by category of business, research, academic. They should also look for jobs not advertised specifically as physics jobs, but which mention the need for science

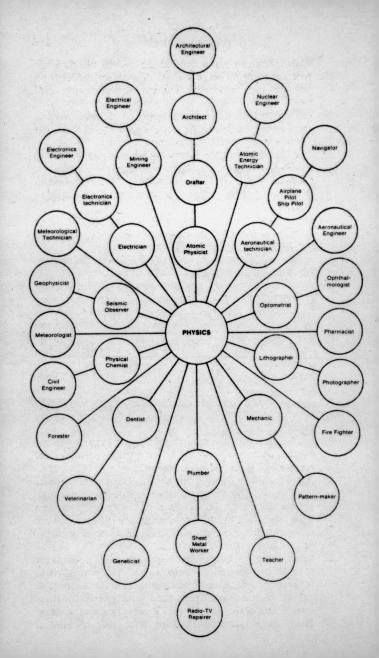

skills. They can make another list of jobs of this kind.

10. Ask a student to make a chart of a career ladder for a physicist in a medical instrument manufacturing company.

11. Ask interested students to write to the professional associations to obtain a code of ethics. Discuss the implications for ethics in science class.

12. Ask the students to look in your school and community libraries for the trade magazines and journals listed on pages 52–54 for physics-related careers. They can make a list of ways in which any particular magazine may be helpful.

13. Have your students write a science article for three different kinds of audiences, based on their reading of the science magazines they find.

14. Make a chart showing the career ladder in college teaching.

15. Have the class look at the classified ads in a trade magazine to see what kinds of jobs are available, what qualifications are required for applicants, and what is being published. They can report to the class on job market trends.

16. Ask the class to make a list of five books that include a physicist.

17. Create a bulletin board on physicists' careers for your classroom.

18. Study the nuclear reactor. Show the many jobs needed to form a reactor—from the construction worker to the nuclear physicist.

19. Study the environmental problems connected with the present-day reactor and the work fields open in the technological end of the problem.

20. After you have covered the development of electronics up through the vacuum tube, explain how through chemical reaction the transistor can replace the vacuum tube. Bring out the advances made and the jobs that are now available in communications and space. Discuss the idea of miniaturization.

21. Study color and how technology has made it possible for it to be transmitted in radio waves. Ask your class to make an investigation of jobs available in the technological end of television. Study the training needs for these jobs. Explain the physics of TV reception to the class.

22. Have the music teacher bring a number of musical

instruments to class during a study of acoustics in physics. A comparison of stringed, woodwind, percussion, and brass instruments in terms of how sound is produced and modulated opens up many fields of discussion and investigation.

23. Ask each student to calculate the BTU ratings of their home for an air-conditioning system. Discuss how their BTU ratings are related to the careers of a) a drafter of the blueprint, b) a research physicist determining the size of the walls, c) an air conditioning engineer, d) an air conditioner designer, e) the installation workers, f) sheet metal workers, and g) the air conditioner repairers.

24. Discuss the differences and similarities in the skills, aptitudes, interests, training time, pay, work environment, and prestige of an electrical engineer and an electrician.

SPECIAL MATERIALS FOR SPECIAL GROUPS

Gifted Students

Who Are the Gifted?

Gifted children are those with demonstrated and potential ability in any of the following areas, singly or in combination:

1. General intellectual ability
2. Specific academic aptitude
3. Creative or productive thinking
4. Leadership ability
5. Visual or performing arts talent
6. Psycho-motor ability

Many of the students seeking advice from teachers about their careers are gifted people, but more talented students deserve encouragement from their teachers to consider career possibilities.

The widespread lack of knowledge about gifted students became painfully evident when a U.S. Office of Education survey revealed that almost half of the school administrators contacted believed that their student bodies contained *no* gifted students. Yet based on the 1970 census, the ERIC Clearinghouse on Handicapped and Gifted Children indicated that from three to five percent of our school-aged children should be classified as having exceptional ability in at least one area, if not in many. Of this group of 2,580,000 students, only about four percent receive even the most minimal attention from schools.

Identification

Gifted youngsters do not inevitably surface. Identification, particularly at the secondary school level, is sometimes difficult due to earlier pressure on very bright or creative students to conform to the prevailing norms set by family and peers. In many cases, students' concerns about seeming "different" have effectively disguised their special aptitudes and abilities. Therefore, many screening methods may be necessary to determine who the gifted are, so that they can benefit from special courses, programs, and counseling.

Group intelligence tests, the most common procedure, are inadequate as the sole means of identification because studies have determined that these tests ignore large numbers of truly capable students. The U.S. Office of Education report on the *Education of the Gifted and Talented* states: "The most highly gifted children were penalized most by group scores; that is, the higher the ability, the greater probability the group test would overlook such ability."

Actual performance is often a better predictor of talent than aptitude and ability tests, especially in visual arts, music, dance, and theater. However, underachievement by talented students is a serious problem and is particularly apparent in four segments of the school population: blacks and other minorities, young women, rural students, and unmotivated white urban males.

Rather than relying on any one method of identification, teachers can integrate a combination of cognitive, affective, and psycho-motor data. Some of the most widely used criteria include:

—Teacher ratings
—Parental judgment
—Students' self-selection (peer ratings)
—Tests (aptitude, creativity, intelligence, achievement, and personality)
—Student's product and performance (writing, art, and acting)
—Grades
—Motivation and self-discipline
—Counseling

Teachers

The teacher's role in identifying and guiding talented students is paramount. The following questions can help students in the process of self-assessment in relation to career exploration:

—How do I feel about being classified as very bright, very talented?

—What problems does it cause?

—What advantages does it offer?

—How do my friends and family encourage or discourage me?

—What are my plans? educational? occupational? Are they realistic?

—How do I hope to attain them?

—What do I do in my leisure time?

—What are my views about specific moral and ethical issues?

—What are my strengths? limitations? weaknesses?

—What kinds of stereotypes do I hold about occupations?

—What are my personal and work values?

Beyond self-evaluation, the teacher can help gifted students in other ways:

1. Indirectly, the teacher may intervene with other teachers and parents who need help in communicating with these youngsters.

2. Direct assistance may take the form of recommending courses as well as teachers whose methods encourage optimum initiative and learning.

3. The teacher should also suggest elective courses and extracurricular activities that broaden and challenge the interests and aptitudes of individual students, including art, music, drama, math, and science.

4. The teacher might be instrumental in getting the school to give or substitute credit for out-of-school lessons or experiences.

Most schools are unable to fulfill the wide-ranging and sometimes advanced needs and abilities of gifted students; therefore, educators must know the available community resources for augmenting student development. For example, relationships with adults from the community can provide both role models and personalized occupational information. The U.S. Office of Education affirms this view: "Evidence from school systems in which they [gifted students] have been given opportunities to work with specialists of similar interests and to explore occupations indicates strongly that career education is of great value in allowing gifted students to assess career options and in motivating them."

Sometimes local colleges allow students to attend regular classes for high school credits or offer special programs on Saturdays, after school, or during summers. Regional theaters, orchestras, and museums are a few of the places that provide performance and learning opportunities for secondary school students. Specialized public schools and programs as well as camps exist for this purpose also. Occupational sites provide places for field trips and volunteer or paid experiences. Usually, these community resources are eager to help students who are genuinely interested; therefore, the teacher needs to know available programs, people, and places.

Special Programs

Two outstanding national programs for gifted students are the Presidential Scholars Program and the Exploration Scholarship Program. The first provides 121 senior high school students, identified by their S.A.T. scores, with a two-day trip to Washington to meet the President and watch the federal government in action.

Teachers who have exceptionally able and interested students in the fields of anthropology and archaeology can write to the regional U.S. Office of Education for application forms to the Exploration Scholarship Program, whose thrust is scientific exploration. Over 150 students spend from one to eight weeks in various areas of the world. There are special categories of winners from the following groups: Bureau of Indian Affairs, Model Cities Youth, Explorer Boy Scouts, and general senior high school students.

National and State Resources

The teacher wanting to know more about helping gifted students can obtain information from the following agencies:

American Association for Gifted Children, Inc., 15 Gramercy Park, New York, New York 10003.

Council for Exceptional Children, 1920 Association Drive, Reston, Virginia 22091.

ERIC Clearinghouse on Handicapped and Gifted Children, 1920 Association Drive, Reston, Virginia 22091.

Foundation for Gifted and Creative Children, 395 Diamond

Hill Road, Warwick, Rhode Island 02886.

National Association for Gifted Children, 8080 Springvalley Drive, Cincinnati, Ohio 45236.

Three periodicals devoted to the needs of gifted students are:

Exceptional Children
Creative Child and Adult Quarterly
Gifted Children Newsletter

Workshops and information are available from:

National/State Leadership Training Institute on the Gifted and the Talented, Civic Center Tower Building, 316 West Second Street, Los Angeles, California 90012.

Every state and territory now has at least one individual designated as the contact person connected with the education of gifted students. These individuals can be contacted through the list of USOE regional offices that concludes this chapter. The lists are maintained by:

Office of Gifted and Talented, U.S. Office of Education, ROB #3, 7th and D Streets, N.W., Washington, D.C. 20202, (202) 245-2482.

The Office of Gifted and Talented has funds available to support state and local education agencies in special programs aimed at gifted and talented students. The Office of Career Education, at the same address, sets aside some funding for career education programs for gifted students.

U.S. Office of Education Regional Offices Programs for the Gifted

Region I	Dr. Harvey Liebergott
Connecticut	USOE/DHEW
Maine	John F. Kennedy Federal
Massachusetts	Building
New Hampshire	Government Center
Rhode Island	Boston, Massachusetts 02203
Vermont	(617) 223-5655

Region II
Canal Zone
New Jersey
New York
Puerto Rico
Virgin Islands

Commsr. Robert H. Seitzer
USOE/DHEW
Federal Building
26 Federal Plaza
New York, New York 10007
(212) 264-4370

Region III
Delaware
District of Columbia
Maryland
Pennsylvania
Virginia
West Virginia

Mr. Albert C. Crambert
USOE/DHEW
P.O. Box 13716
Philadelphia, Pennsylvania 19101
(215) 597-1033

Region IV
Alabama
Florida
Georgia
Kentucky
Mississippi
North Carolina
South Carolina
Tennessee

Miss Ellen Lyles
USOE/DHEW
Peachtree-Seventh Building
50 7th Street, N.E., Room 404
Atlanta, Georgia 30323
(404) 526-5311

Region V
Illinois
Indiana
Michigan
Minnesota
Ohio
Wisconsin

Dr. Richard Naber
USOE/DHEW
300 South Wacker Drive
32nd Floor
Chicago, Illinois 60606
(312) 353-1743

Region VI
Arkansas
Louisiana
New Mexico
Oklahoma
Texas

Mr. Edward J. Baca
USOE/DHEW
1114 Commerce Street
Dallas, Texas 75202
(214) 749-2634

Region VII
Iowa
Kansas
Missouri

Dr. Harold Blackburn
USOE/DHEW
Federal Office Building

Nebraska	601 East 12th Street
	Kansas City, Missouri 64106
	(816) 374-2276

Region VIII

Colorado	Dr. Edward B. Larsh
Montana	USOE/DHEW
North Dakota	Federal Office Building
South Dakota	19th and Stout Streets
Utah	Denver, Colorado 80202
Wyoming	(303) 837-3676

Region IX

Arizona	Mrs. Maryanne Faris
California	USOE/DHEW
Hawaii	Federal Office Building
Nevada	50 Fulton Street
American Samoa	San Francisco, California 94102
Guam	(415) 556-7750

Region X

Alaska	Mr. Robert Radford
Idaho	USOE/DHEW
Oregon	Arcade Plaza Building
Washington	1321 Second Avenue, MS-628
	Seattle, Washington 98101
	(206) 442-0460

Physically Disabled Students

The question, "What will—indeed, what can—I do after graduation from high school?" is of special concern to the disabled student and his or her family. Despite advances in recent years, the career outlook for the more severely physically disabled is still not an entirely good one. To a far greater extent than their nondisabled peers they are involuntarily unemployed or underemployed. Such a lack of employment opportunities is an unnecessary loss both to the disabled themselves and to society at large. Society's goal should be to seek to make work possible, meaningful, and satisfying for all students.

Too often we are satisfied when we have found something that a handicapped person can do. Instead we should be dissatisfied until and unless we have explored, to the fullest possible extent, the total array of work that might be possible for, and meaningful to, a given handicapped person.

Although there are special factors to consider when implementing career development programs with physically disabled students, the basic components of the process are equally applicable to both the nondisabled and the disabled.

The greatest difference in the career development for the disabled is that their choices may be more circumscribed because of the handicap imposed by their physical limitations. Expressed in slightly different terms, the physical disability may impose an *occupational* handicap, that is, the person is not succeeding or cannot be expected to succeed in a regular training program or on the job and the person's disability is a contributing factor to his lack of success. Such an actual or potential handicap need not be a permanent condition but can often be overcome by specialized training, equipment, and devices; by medical restoration; and by guidance and placement services.

Restricted Work-related and Social Experiences

A characteristic of some physically disabled young persons is that they will have had few of the work-related and social experiences that nondisabled children and adolescents have had. As a result they may be immature, lacking in self-confidence, or unrealistic in their career aspirations. Some may have aspirations that are too low—others have aspirations that are too high. This lack of experience places disabled students at a severe disadvantage compared to their nondisabled peers.

Background of Educational Handicap

Educational retardation may be directly related to physical disability rather than to mental limitations. A student may be capable of higher education despite her grade point average or standardized test score results. This is especially true of hearing-impaired students, for whom verbal ability and reading scores are *not* synonymous with intelligence. A student with an educational handicap needs assistance in remediation and in selecting higher education institutions that include preparatory or remedial courses and services as part of the total curriculum.

Analysis of Physical Limitations

A major premise in helping disabled students is to concentrate on abilities rather than limitations. Comprehensive, up-to-date medical data from the physician is essential for career planning. The ideal goal of career development is participation in an occupation in which the physical disability does not constitute a handicap. A prerequisite of career adjustment is to know the precise limitations of the disability in terms of the physical capacities of the student and in terms of the environmental conditions that should be avoided. Four major factors involved in the successful employment of disabled workers are:

—The worker should have the ability to accomplish the task efficiently.
—The worker should not be a hazard to himself.
—The worker must not jeopardize the safety of others.
—The job should not aggravate the disability or handicap of the worker.

Avoidance of Job Stereotypes

Educators often compile a list of jobs that are suitable for persons with a particular disability, e.g., the deaf as printers, the blind as dictaphone typists, the orthopedically impaired as shoe repairers. Stereotyping the disabled limits their opportunities and aspirations. Physically disabled persons display as wide a variety of aptitudes, interests, and life-style preferences as do nondisabled persons! This does not mean that a teacher should not be aware of the types of jobs that have been successfully performed by disabled persons. Such information, especially if coupled with details regarding special devices and techniques utilized, is needed to widen the range of careers for the disabled student.

Danger of Overeducation

Close to the job stereotype danger is the assumption that disabled students should have a four-year college education— "the more education the better" syndrome. Just as with the nondisabled, not all disabled persons desire to have or can profit from a university education. Education beyond high school need not be limited to a four-year college degree. Nor does a decision not to attend a four-year college relegate a person to a boring, dead end job. An increasing number of vocational-technical education programs for the hearing-impaired have been started within the past ten years. See the references at the end of this chapter for guides to technical education.

Problems of Unrealistic Goals

Unfortunately, the abilities, limitations, and interests of the disabled student are not the only factors to be considered in determining whether or not a career goal is realistic. Union policies and employment practices are also involved. Despite job development activities on the part of rehabilitation professionals and disabled persons themselves, such barriers still exist and will continue to do so. As part of the career education program, therefore, the student must be informed about such potential barriers as certification and licensure requirements as they relate to individuals with physical disabilities.

Another question that arises is: Should employability be the major factor dictating whether a student should pursue a certain program in high school or in higher education? Assuming that it is possible for a severely disabled student to complete a certain career program, and that she is realistically aware that securing employment will be difficult, should it not be the student who decides whether or not to pursue the career program? The student's right to self-determination, in this case as in all others, cannot be overlooked.

Further Reading

Boule, Frank. *Handicapping America,* Harper & Row, 10 East 53rd Street, New York, New York, 10022, $10.95.

Braille and large-type books on occupational guidance, vocations, and trades. Louisville, Kentucky: American Printing House for the Blind, P.O. Box 6085, KY 40206, 1974. Free.

Lacey, David W. "Career Development of Deaf Youngsters," in *New Thrusts in Education of the Deaf,* pp. 3–9, National Technical Institute for the Deaf, 1 Lomb Memorial Drive, Rochester, NY 14623, 1973. Free.

Mitchell, Joyce Slayton. *The Work Book: A Guide to Skilled Jobs*, Bantam Books, 666 Fifth Ave., New York, NY 10019.

Pettingil, Don G. *Concept of a Work Study Program for Hearing Impaired High School Students*. Reprint available free from author: Don G. Pettingil, White House Conference on Handicapped, 1832 M Street, NW, Ste. 801, Washington, DC 20036.

Teacher's Manual: A Course in Career Decision-making for Special Education. ERIC Document Reproduction Service, Box 190, Arlington, VA 22210. ED Number 091 560. Hard copy, $9.95. Microfiche, 76 cents.

Vocational Education Resource Materials/Handicapped and Special Education. Educational Instructional Materials Center, University of Wisconsin, Teacher Education Building, Room 180, 225 North Mills Street, Madison, WI 53706.

Wright, Beatrice. *The Question Still Stands: Should a Person Be Realistic?* in *Rehabilitation Counseling Bulletin*, 1968, 11 (4), pp. 291–296.

Women and Nonwhite Students

Sexism and racism, both in education and in employment, are against the law. But in a society where white males are considered the norm and everyone else must adapt as best they can, racism and sexism are practiced both at school and at work. Getting a job, getting equal pay for equal work, getting equal work, getting promoted, and getting laid off are easy ways to measure how discrimination works. In all cases, women and nonwhite workers are at the lowest end of the scale.

Employment and education laws are now on the side of minorities and women. But, in order to test the law or to push for compliance with the law, women and minorities must aspire to careers traditionally followed by white males, such as those of securities salesperson, veterinarian, systems analyst, dentist, new car dealer, agricultural economist, and geologist. Helping students to aspire to careers that are nontraditional for those of their sex or ethnic background is a responsibility of all educators who say they are interested in student growth.

Basic Cultural Assumptions

In its excellent publication *Racism in Career Education Materials*, the Council on Interracial Books for Children provides the following basic assumptions concerning racism in career education materials: that ours is a society in which racial minorities and women do not receive an equitable share of high-status, decision-making positions with commensurate salaries, and social, economic, and political benefits; and that any form of education that does not directly address itself to correcting this inequality is, per se, sexist and racist and any career education materials that fail to address this inequity are to be labeled racist and sexist in content.

The importance of detecting and correcting every instance of sexism and racism in career education materials cannot be overly stressed. The concept of career education has been a source of controversy among Third World and feminist educators since its introduction in 1970. The controversy has centered around the potential misuse of career education as an exclusionary device to "track" minority and female students from high-status positions into lower level technical, clerical, and blue-collar jobs, thereby reinforcing the already unequal distribution of income and status in our society. Given this controversy, anyone examining career education materials must be made aware of the need to take a hard look at the underlying educational and social assumptions found in such materials.

Because sexism and racism are often covertly present in communications of all types, educators must be particularly sensitive to hidden and subtle messages embedded in both words and illustrations used in instructional materials. Therefore, an intensive analysis of all written and visual content is recommended when selecting any materials for school use. Moreover, when such materials have been specifically designed for use in career education curricula, it is critical that any selection committee include minority and female group representatives in order to augment sensitivity to the issue of employment discrimination. It is also recommended that a fundamental understanding of the patterns of institutional racism and sexism in education and labor at the national and local levels should be required in all selectors of career education materials.

White women have another subtle barrier to hurdle before they get to serious career decision making. The basic assumption in our middle- and working-class white society that a man must be the financial provider for a woman has devastating implications on the career development of young women. The notion that a man's masculinity and identity are tied to the amount of money he makes and the kind of life-style he can provide for a wife and family underlies the fear a young woman has about making more money than her husband, about having a higher career status than her husband. Our stories and myths punish achieving women by denying them love.

Effective teaching against sexism does *not* mean role reversal. Getting more men into nursing and more women into engineering is not the crucial task. The crucial task for educators dealing with sexism is to change the basic assumption that girls and women will be financially protected: if not by their fathers, then by their husbands; if not by their husbands, then by the state. The U.S. Department of Labor documents very well the fact that women are financially responsible for themselves *and* for their children. The shocking increase in single parent families (97% are females) in the last two years is being ignored by educators. When young women finally see themselves as having to financially support their families, their commitment to career decisions will be different.

Strategies for Change

White educators have had problems recognizing and coming to grips with covert racism in educational materials. Future efforts to make career education materials more relevant to minorities should, at the outset, involve Third World people in program planning, preparation of materials, implementation of programs, and evaluation of programs and materials.

The concerns of educators about the bias against minorities in career education materials must be brought to the attention of publishers and manufacturers. Certainly, educational leadership is required if publishers are to succeed in making their products antiracist, antisexist, and more humanistic generally. Teachers, boards of education, principals, guidance counselors, and curriculum specialists must all play the role of advocates for the interests of all learners.

If the real goal of career education is to make education more relevant to future work experience, then resources outside the school environment must be utilized in strengthening curricula. The expertise of minority people who work in government, labor unions, and civil-rights organizations is available to school authorities and should be sought. In addition, input from groups with special concerns like the Association for Non-White Careers in Personnel and Guidance could be extremely useful.

While the exploration of outside resources may involve long-range planning, other strategies to overcome racist content in materials currently in use can be implemented immediately by classroom personnel.

1. Good use can be made of essentially bad materials. Teachers can use racist connotations uncovered in career education material as discussion stimulators toward learning more about the nature of institutional racism and its manifestations. From the earliest grades through college, well-informed and well-intentioned adults (including parents) can guide students in examining and critiquing materials. In small or large group discussions, questions such as these might be explored:

   —Which minority groups were shown in this material?
   —Were their roles presented to reflect the current realities of society or to reflect society as it ought to be? In either case, did the text (or film commentary) discuss injustice to minorities?
   —What might the author or film producer have done to show this minority group in a more positive way?
   —What three things would have been different if all of the white people were shown as blacks, for instance, and all of the minorities as whites?
   —Can you see why it is especially important for minorities to consider more professional careers rather than just jobs?

2. Teachers, particularly, have a responsibility to help students develop a greater awareness of the problem of discrimination in employment. In addition to arranging classroom presentations by employment counselors or workers, teachers ought to consider visits by affirmative action officers or minority persons involved in combating employment discrimination.

3. Students engaged in researching career opportunities should be encouraged to look into the historical involvement of minorities in a particular occupation and relate their findings to future job prospects. Areas of special impact like construction or communications,

where legislation or government policies are slowly being developed to insure minority access, should be presented, along with other pertinent information regarding jobs in that field.

4. Teachers should be on the lookout for dead end jobs presented in career education materials. Technological advancement is changing the nature of many jobs and virtually eliminating others. Hence, preparation and training information should focus on jobs that are not likely to change radically or become obsolete, and should aim at maximizing opportunities to qualify for several occupations and not aim at encouraging limited training for a job that might not exist in the next decade. In addition, there is also the problem of the relatively short life cycle of many jobs that require nontransferable skills.

5. Of course, all schools should be actively involved in examining the issues of our time and countering undemocratic practices inside and outside the school environment. Racism awareness training for school personnel ought to include:

—Analysis of cultural clashes in the classroom— causes, effects, and alternatives.
—Development of teacher sensitivity to racial issues.
—Development of methods for screening textbooks and other materials for racism.

A Classroom Learning Strategy

I. Investigate the realities of racism and sexism in the community.

II. Design a racist- and sexist-free business enterprise.

I. Have the class break up into a few groups with each group responsible for gathering information about a different business in the community, i.e., newspaper, bank, factory, department store.

1. Each group should find out the answers to as many of the following questions as possible:

What is the percentage of white males among the owners? The board of directors? The top executives? The lesser executives? The sales staff? The secretaries and clerks? The skilled work force? The unskilled work force? The janitors and cleaners?

2. What are the salaries of the above jobs?

3. How are new employees hired? Through word-of-mouth recommendations by present employees? Through job advertisements? In what newspapers? Is the test or qualification requirement for the job relevant to the actual work? What color and sex is the person who conducts job interviews?

4. How are employees promoted? Who decides on the criteria? Is there on-the-job training? Are decisions of promotion, pay increments, and layoffs based on seniority ("last hired, first fired") or on a recognition of past discrimination and a desire to compensate for it through affirmative action?

5. Are all supervisors required to be sensitive to cultural differences? Are they trained in this regard?

6. Does the business use any minority suppliers or services? What percentage?

7. Is the business located in a spot that is easily reached by minority workers? If not, are minority employees compensated for the extra travel required of them because of residential segregation?

8. If the business makes any charitable contributions, what percentage goes to minority and women's causes?

9. What efforts, if any, has the business made to be antiracist and antisexist?

10. What color and sex is the person(s) who has the power to decide: Who is hired and fired? Who is promoted? Who gets paid how much? Who the suppliers are? How profits are divided? How fast or hard people work? What the paid holidays are?

    When each group reports their findings, discussion might include a comparison to the national picture.

II. Designing a sexist- and racist-free enterprise should be a freewheeling activity based upon group discussion, with consensus, if possible, of values, goals, and methods.

What is important here is for the students to reflect on our society's practices, on how they undercut our professed ideals, and on what can be done to redress any perceived injustice.

Crucial Definitions

Racism—Sexism:

—Sexist and racist materials—materials that in some way demonstrate the superiority of white males at the expense of Third World people and women.

—Nonracist and nonsexist materials—materials that do not demonstrate the superiority of white males, but also do not move our present sexist-racist society a step toward full opportunity and equality of all people.

—Antiracist and antisexist materials—materials that take definite steps toward full realization of opportunity, justice, and equality, and attempt to reverse patterns of institutional racism.

Segregation—the separation or isolation of individuals and groups from a larger group or from society as: the separation or isolation by race, sex, class, or ethnic group by enforced or voluntary residence in a restricted area, barriers to social intercourse, divided educational facilities, sports, classes, or other discriminatory means.

Desegregation—in reference to the content of educational materials, this term means the *inclusion* of specific information about the history, culture, and life-styles of female and nonwhite groups in all aspects of study.

Ethnocentrism—a tendency toward viewing alien cultures with disfavor and a resulting sense of inherent superiority.

Stereotype—something repeated or reproduced without variation: something conforming to a fixed or general pattern and lacking individual distinguishing marks or qualities, especially a standardized mental picture held in common by members of a group and representing an oversimplified opinion, affective attitude, or uncritical judgment.

Third World people—those people of ethnic or national origins historically oppressed by nations of the first and second worlds. The first world refers to the British Empire and other European colonists including the United States; the second world refers to the Soviet Union and its satellite nations. Third World people, a minority in the United States but a majority of the world's population, are of African, Asian, Latin, and Native American descent.

Track(ing)—one of two or more courses of study covering the same general field usually at different levels of intensity and offered by a school to meet the diverse needs of particular groups of students.

More to Read

1. CIBC, *Racism in Career Education Materials*, Council on Interracial Books for Children, 1841 Broadway, New York, NY 10023 ($2.50).

   A study, based on one hundred randomly selected career education materials, of how to detect racism and how to counteract its effects in the classroom.

2. CIBC, *Interracial Books for Children*.

   This bulletin offers incisive evaluations of trade books and textbooks for children with special emphasis on racist and sexist values. It also suggests sources for alternative materials for home and classroom (above address). The best antiracism resource for educators.

3. *Cracking The Glass Slipper: Peer's Guide to Ending Sex Bias in Your Schools.*, Peer, 1029 Vermont Avenue, N.W., Suite 800, Washington, D.C. 20005 (1977).

   A kit of materials which tell you how to review your school for sexism—step by step. Contains review guides for athletics, vocational education, counseling, rules and customs, the pregnant student, a title IX primer and resource materials. Designed especially for high schools, the kit is an excellent source for teachers.

4. Downs, Anthony, *Racism in American and How to Combat It*. U.S. Commission on Civil Rights, Washington, DC 20425.

   This publication is the place to start a study of racism. It has a good definition of racism and a unique six pages on "How Racism Provides Benefits to Whites." Downs also writes on basic strategies for combating racism; although not mentioning education specifically, he explains strategies that can be applied to educational institutions.

5. Katz, Michael B., *Class, Bureaucracy and Schools: The Illusion of Educational Change in America*. New York: Praeger (1971).

   This small book represents a real departure from traditional educational history in that it raises questions about the covert functions of the institutional practices of education. An important book for teachers.

6. Disch, Robert, and Schwartz, Barry N., *White Racism:*

Its History, Pathology and Practice. New York: Dell Publishing Co. (1970).

Articles written by both blacks and whites document the existence of racism. A wide range of diversified materials is covered. Good discussion of the effects of racial bias in textbooks on white students (Young and Soloman article).

7. Knowles, Louis, and Prewitt, Kenneth, *Institutional Racism in America.* Englewood Cliffs: Prentice-Hall (1969).

A classic in racism literature, this book gives an explanation of the ideological roots of racism in America. It also dramatically illustrates the institutional racism perpetrated by political, economic, legal, health and welfare, religious, and educational institutions. A must!

8. Mitchell, Joyce Slayton, *Other Choices for Becoming a Woman: A Handbook to Help High School Women Make Decisions.* Dell (1975).

This unique feminist handbook was written to help young women realize their potential in today's world where their roles are changing so rapidly. In particular, it is designed to encourage high school women to make plans while they are still in school in order to realize the wide range of careers and life-styles from which they can choose. No door need automatically be closed to a young woman trying to make the right decisions in education, religion, sex, friendship, sports, careers, arts, and leisure.

9. Mitchell, Joyce Slayton, *Free to Choose: Decision Making for Young Men.* Dell (1977).

This important and timely book is the companion volume to *Other Choices for Becoming a Woman.* Its purpose is to assist high school men by helping them to understand the many choices open to them in developing all the facets of their lives, so that they are not bound by traditional and stereotypic views of men. The author encourages young men to value their own experiences and feelings of self-discovery rather than to follow cultural expectations. Mitchell discusses ways to break out of traditional sexist roles in friendship, love and marriage, religion, sports, and careers and advises young men to trust their own visions of themselves as their experiences and feelings grow. This is the only young men's liberation book to date, and the contributors include the foremost male liberationists—Warren Farrell, author of *The Liberated Man*, and Marc Feigen-Fasteau, who wrote *The Male Machine*.

10. Mitchell, Joyce Slayton, *I Can Be Anything: Careers and Colleges for Young Women*. The College Board (1978), Bantam (1978).

I Can Be Anything is designed solely for women. It provides readers with a candid look at what each career is really like, including on-the-job interviews with women from every part of the country. In addition, for each occupation, information is provided on how many women are employed—and where, on the starting and experienced salaries, employment prospects, colleges that award the most degrees to women, and on where to get more information about the field.

Each career has a listing of the cluster of personal skills required (for instance, it takes physical stamina to be an actress, neatness to be a dental hygienist, good speaking and writing abilities to be a political scientist).

The book is illustrated with 38 photographs of women at work. 336 pages.

11. Stacey, J., and Daniels, Bereand J., *And Jill Came Tumbling After: Sexism in American Education*. Dell (1974).

An anthology that gathered the best available pieces to show how sexism operates at all levels of education. It also suggests how schools can be reformed to allow both girls *and* boys to pursue their individual interests and fulfill their potential. If you don't think *your* school is sexist, start here!

12. Ryan, William, *Blaming the Victim*. New York: Pantheon Books (1971).

A must for all those interested in understanding the way in which white society defines people of color as both the cause and the effect of their circumstances. Written in easy-to-understand language, the book brilliantly exposes some of the myths of racism and social science.

13. Terry, Robert W., *For Whites Only*. Grand Rapids: William R. Berdmans Publishing Co. (1970).

Terry's book largely concerns white racism in industry. However, few books give so clear an exposure of the processes of racism—the liberal who will not see blacks as individuals, the conservative who will not see blacks as a group. There is an outline of basic strategies for bringing change in our society, including educational institutions. It is one of the few "how to" books for those determined to follow a new white consciousness.

14. Yette, Samuel F., *The Choice: The Issue of Black Survival in America.* New York: Berkley Medallion Books (1971).

This book is an important one for developing an analysis of racism in American society. It deals with the issues around the forced obsolescence of blacks in America and defines survival as the primary issue facing blacks in this country.